Divine Wealth
Aligning Faith, Wisdom, and Purpose to Create True Abundance
Philosophy

Divine Wealth

Copyright © 2025

All rights reserved. No part of this publication may be reproduced, distributed, or transmitted in any form or by any means, including photocopying, recording, or other electronic or mechanical methods, without the prior written permission of the publisher, except in the case of brief quotations embodied in critical reviews and certain other noncommercial uses permitted by copyright law.

ISBN 978-1-7642508-2-5 (paperback)
ISBN 978-1-7642508-3-2 (ebook)

Printed via Kindle Direct Publishing

Divine Wealth

Contents

Contents

Preface 5
Prologue: The Whisper at Offering Time 6
Chapter 1: God's Blueprint for Abundance 12
Chapter 2: Faith in Action: Stepping Into the Flow of Divine Provision 26
Chapter 3: The Power of Stewardship: Multiplying What God Has Placed in Your Hands 39
Chapter 4: The Kingdom Law of Increase: How God Expands What You Believe For 53
Chapter 5: The Currency of Faith: Living in Heaven's Economy on Earth 66
Chapter 6: The Law of Divine Timing: Trusting God's Pace for Your Prosperity 80
Chapter 7: The Anointing of Increase: Walking in Divine Provision and Overflow 93
Chapter 8: The Faith to Build: Constructing Wealth Through Vision, Work, and Worship 107
Chapter 9: Harvest of the Heart, Reaping God's Abundance Through Generosity and Grace 119
Chapter 10: The Anointing of Increase, Walking in Divine Prosperity Without Losing Your Purpose 129
Chapter 11: The Covenant of Contentment, Finding Joy and Purpose in Every Season of Provision 141
Chapter 12: The Power of Kingdom Partnership, How Collective Faith Creates Unstoppable Impact 152

Divine Wealth

Chapter 13: Legacy and Light, Becoming the Bridge for Future Generations 164

Chapter 14: The Divine Exchange, Where Faith Meets Fruitfulness 175

Epilogue: Walking It Out – Turning Divine Wealth into Real-World Income 180

About the Author 193

Divine Wealth

Preface

This book was born from stillness, from a quiet moment of offering and reflection that became a lifelong revelation. It is not a manual about wealth or success, but a conversation about purpose, stewardship, and creation. It speaks to those who believe that abundance is not merely about possession, but about partnership with something greater.

Every word has been written with prayer and gratitude, with a single desire: that the reader would be reminded that giving and growing are inseparable. True increase begins when we understand that we are not owners, but caretakers, that everything entrusted to us carries both blessing and responsibility.

As you read, may you find the courage to act on what stirs your heart. May these words remind you that your capacity to create is divine, and your ability to give is sacred. And may the insight found within these pages lead not just to personal prosperity, but to a life that continually pours into others.

Divine Wealth

Prologue: The Whisper at Offering Time

Divine Wealth

The room was filled with warmth and light, that familiar glow that settles over a Sunday service just before the message. The air carried a quiet hum of expectancy, people were smiling, whispering, praying. It was the kind of atmosphere where you can feel faith hanging in the air, alive and steady.

I stood there, phone in hand, preparing to make my usual transfer for tithes and offerings. Around me, others reached for their envelopes, and the ushers moved with the calm rhythm of service. The pastor spoke gently about generosity, about how giving isn't an act of loss but of love. "We don't give because we have to," he said, "we give because we get to."

I smiled, I'd heard that phrase many times before. But for some reason, that morning it landed differently. It lingered in my heart long after the words had passed. I looked down at my screen, entered the amount, and hovered over the "confirm" button. And right there, in the middle of that ordinary, familiar moment, a thought came to me, quiet but strong, clear but unforced:

"How can I give more?"

It wasn't guilt. It wasn't ambition. It was curiosity, holy curiosity. A question that came from a place of gratitude and longing. How could I give more to God? More to His work, His people, His purposes? How could I make my offering more than a number on a screen? Before I could even answer myself, another thought followed. It wasn't from me. It was something deeper, something that felt placed in my spirit rather than formed in my mind:

"To give more, you must first learn how to create more."

I froze. The room around me faded for a moment. I wasn't hearing a voice out loud, but it was undeniable, a whisper with weight. It was as if heaven had leaned close to say, "I will bless what you give, but I also want to bless what you build."

In that instant, I knew that God wasn't just challenging my generosity, He was expanding my understanding. He wasn't asking

Divine Wealth

me to give more of what I already had, He was inviting me to grow into someone who could create more, so that I could give freely and abundantly.

I realised that day that I had been faithful, but I hadn't been fruitful. I had learned to give, but not to multiply.

As I pressed "transfer," something in me shifted. It wasn't a transaction, it was transformation. I had made offerings countless times before, but this was different. This time, I wasn't just sending money, I was surrendering limitation.

A thought formed clearly in my heart:

"My people know how to give, but many have not learned how to grow."

It came like revelation, an understanding that God's people often have passion without preparation, generosity without growth. We pray for abundance, but we don't always study how to sustain it. We long to give more, yet feel unqualified or unequipped to generate more.

That day, I felt God commission me to help change that. Not through a sermon, not through a lecture, but through a calling, to teach Christians how to prosper His way.

I didn't rush to write it down. I didn't announce it. I just stood there, letting that revelation settle in my heart. And as I did, I knew this wasn't an idea, it was an assignment.

I made a covenant with God right then. I said, "If You give me the wisdom, I will give You the work. If You provide the message, I will make it an offering."

This book is the fruit of that covenant. It was born out of that single, sacred moment, a whisper that became a mission.

From that day forward, I made a promise: every profit from this book will be my tithe. Every word will be written as an act of worship. I will use what He gives me to give back to Him.

Divine Wealth

And I invite every reader who is blessed through it to join me in that same heart posture. Whatever increase this message brings, whether in income, opportunities, or ideas, take a portion and return it to God. Let this book become a movement of giving that multiplies across lives and generations. Because when we commit to make generosity our lifestyle, not our limit, heaven keeps the flow open.
That day changed my understanding of what it means to be blessed. I saw that God's desire is not just to fill our hands, but to shape our hearts. He doesn't simply want us to receive abundance, He wants us to reveal it. To become reflections of His creativity, His stewardship, His generosity.
For too long, many of us have separated faith from finance, treating money as something less spiritual. But that morning, I saw clearly, God is not silent about wealth, He has principles for it. He doesn't condemn provision, He commands stewardship. He is not against prosperity, He is against idolatry.
Wealth, when handled with wisdom, is worship. Abundance, when surrendered to God, is obedience. And generosity, when practiced with intention, becomes a form of ministry.
It became clear to me that the same God who teaches us to pray also teaches us to produce. The same One who commands us to tithe also gives us the power to create wealth . That morning, I understood that the "power to create wealth" is not just skill or luck, it's revelation. It's the wisdom to align our spiritual lives with our practical lives, to live in a way that both honours God and transforms the world around us.
That revelation began in stillness. No lights, no grandeur, just a quiet moment between God and me. And from that quiet, this book was born.
This isn't a book about getting rich for pride's sake, it's about understanding that prosperity, when guided by purpose, is holy. It's about seeing wealth not as a prize but as a platform. It's about freeing

Divine Wealth

Christians from guilt around success, and showing that money is not evil when it serves a righteous mission.

I realised that morning that my tithe wasn't supposed to be the ceiling of my generosity, it was the foundation. It wasn't the finish line of giving, it was the starting point of stewardship.

That's what this book is about, Divine Wealth. It's about learning to align spiritual principles with practical action. It's about combining faith, wisdom, and purpose to create impact. It's about transforming the way we think about money so that we can transform what money does through us.

As I walked out of church that day, I felt lighter, not because I had given, but because I had understood. I knew then that God was calling me not only to worship with my voice, but to worship with my work. To use my mind, my creativity, my discipline, and my diligence as instruments of praise.

Since that moment, I've carried one truth deeply in my spirit, we are not called to chase money. We are called to channel it. We are not called to love wealth. We are called to leverage it. We are not called to hoard resources. We are called to harvest them for the Kingdom.

The ability to create wealth is not a worldly ambition, it is a divine responsibility. It is how we multiply what God gives us and use it to expand His work on earth.

And so, this book is my offering, the written form of that tithe, that promise, that whisper I received during offering time. My prayer is that as you read, you will feel what I felt that morning, that quiet yet undeniable tug of purpose.

May it remind you that giving is not the end of your generosity, it's the beginning of your growth. That when you learn to create with God's wisdom and give with God's heart, you become unstoppable in His purpose.

Divine Wealth

That moment, that single act of worship, that one transfer made with trembling hands, changed the trajectory of my faith. And I believe it can change yours too.

Because the truth is simple, when we align our finances with God's purpose, heaven moves. When we give with understanding, increase follows with intention. And when we see wealth not as possession but as partnership with God, we begin to live out what I call Divine Wealth, abundance that flows not to us, but through us.

This is where it all began, one offering, one whisper, one moment of revelation that would become a lifelong mission.

And I pray that as you read these pages, you hear that same whisper in your own heart:

"To give more, learn to create more. To create more, trust Me."

That is the invitation.

That is the call.

That is the beginning of Divine Wealth.

Divine Wealth

Chapter 1: God's Blueprint for Abundance

Divine Wealth

I left that Sunday with a question still echoing in my heart, How can I give more? But as the days passed, that simple question grew into something much bigger. It became an invitation from God to understand how He designed increase in the first place. I began to see that the issue was not about giving alone, it was about grasping the divine blueprint that governs all abundance.

The more I prayed and reflected, the clearer it became that God never intended His children to live in lack. Scarcity was never part of His design. When He spoke creation into existence, He spoke in the language of abundance. When He said, "Let there be light," He didn't create a flicker; He created a sun that burns with power and beauty. When He gathered the waters, He didn't form a puddle; He formed oceans that roar with life. From the very beginning, God's intention was not just life, but overflow. Everything He made contained within it the potential to multiply. When He blessed Adam and Eve, His first command was, "Be fruitful and multiply." It was not just an instruction, it was identity. To be human was to be fruitful. To walk with God was to live in the rhythm of increase.

That truth began to unravel something deep within me. For so long, I had seen abundance as something external, something to chase or achieve. I thought prosperity was about having more, when in reality, it was about becoming more. Abundance was never something to pursue; it was something to recognise. It was hidden in plain sight, resting in the soil of obedience, gratitude, and faith. God's design was not for us to strive endlessly but to steward faithfully. He does not ask us to create something from nothing; He asks us to cultivate what He has already placed within and around us.

Somewhere along the way, many of us lost sight of that truth. We began to see lack as normal and to treat struggle as holy. We inherited a mindset that confused poverty with purity and abundance with arrogance. But the more I studied Scripture, the more I saw that God is not glorified when His children barely survive. He is glorified when

Divine Wealth

they thrive with integrity and generosity. Jesus Himself said, "I came that they may have life, and have it abundantly." The word "abundantly" means "beyond measure," "overflowing," "more than enough." That is the heartbeat of heaven.

Yet, many of us were raised to feel guilty for wanting more, as if the desire to grow and prosper somehow offended God. But guilt is not holiness; it is hesitation. And hesitation keeps good people small. When we live from scarcity, we see giving as loss, not as planting. We fear generosity because it feels like subtraction. But when we live from abundance, we understand that every seed sown is a down payment on future harvest. Scarcity whispers, "If I give, I'll have less." Abundance declares, "If I sow, I'll grow."

The difference between the two begins in the mind. says, "Do not be conformed to the pattern of this world, but be transformed by the renewing of your mind." For years, I assumed this verse was only about behaviour, but the Spirit revealed something deeper. Renewing your mind is not just about moral purity; it's about financial maturity. It's about learning to think like a steward instead of a struggler, to think like a creator instead of a consumer. The world's pattern is built on fear and control, but God's pattern is built on trust and purpose. The world teaches, "Get all you can and keep it." God teaches, "Use all you have and give it."

To live by God's blueprint, you must unlearn the false ideas that have kept you small: that you're bad with money, that you'll never have enough, that it's wrong to want more, that wealth and faith cannot coexist. These are not humble thoughts; they are lies dressed as modesty. True humility does not reject God's blessings; it redirects them. It says, "Lord, everything I have belongs to You. Use it as You will."

When you begin to renew your mind this way, something shifts inside you. You stop waiting for miracles and start walking in them. You begin to see that abundance is not accidental, it is intentional. It

Divine Wealth

follows obedience, it follows diligence, it follows trust. You discover that heaven has its own economy, one that operates on principles very different from the world's. In the world's economy, value decreases when something is used; in God's economy, value multiplies when something is given.

Every story of divine provision in Scripture follows this principle. When the widow gave her last two coins, she didn't lose, she stepped into overflow. When the boy offered his five loaves and two fish, he didn't deplete his lunch, he fed thousands. When Abraham lifted the knife in obedience, he didn't lose his son, he encountered the God who provides. In heaven's mathematics, the more you release, the more you receive, because in God's hands, giving is never depletion; it is creation.

That's why Jesus could promise, "Give, and it will be given to you, good measure, pressed down, shaken together and running over." When you give according to divine rhythm, you step into the circulation of heaven. You give what you have, God breathes on it, multiplies it, and then trusts you with more. But when fear interrupts that flow, the current stops. When fear controls your finances, you disconnect from divine circulation, but when faith takes over, heaven moves again.

Every economy has its own currency, and in the Kingdom, that currency is faith. Money is just the tool; faith is the transaction. You cannot buy God's favour, but you can believe for it. You cannot purchase His blessing, but you can position yourself to receive it through trust. The woman with the issue of blood did not bring a payment; she brought faith. The centurion who asked for healing did not bring wealth; he brought belief. The disciples who fed thousands did not bring resources; they brought obedience. Faith transforms what you already have into more than enough. That is what abundance truly is , not the absence of need, but the presence of trust.

Divine Wealth

When you trust that God is your source, lack loses its authority over you. You stop looking for provision because you realise you are already standing in it. Living by divine blueprint means trusting the design even when you cannot see the details. The enemy's first lie to humanity was about lack. "Did God really say…?" was not a question of curiosity; it was a seed of doubt meant to distort abundance. He made Adam and Eve believe they were missing something, even though they already had everything. That lie still circulates today. But God's truth remains the same: you are not missing anything you need to begin. You already carry potential within you; faith is what activates it.

The world's blueprint for wealth is built on self-reliance, ambition, and accumulation. God's blueprint is built on stewardship, wisdom, and service. The world says, "Protect what's yours." God says, "Give what's Mine." The world says, "You're successful when you have more." God says, "You're successful when you do more good with what you have." The difference is profound. One creates stress; the other creates peace. When you live according to the world's design, money becomes a master. When you live according to God's, money becomes a messenger.

When you walk in alignment with His principles, you don't have to chase blessings; blessings begin to chase you. Scripture promises, "All these blessings will come upon you and overtake you if you obey the voice of the Lord your God." That word "overtake" means blessings will find you even when you're not looking for them. You cannot outrun what God has ordained for you when you are walking in alignment with His will.

Abundance, then, is not about accumulation, it's about assignment. God gives increase to those He can trust with influence. When your heart is aligned with purpose, increase will always find you. But when your heart is ruled by pride, increase will only reveal what was hidden within you all along. Wealth is never random; it's relational. It flows

Divine Wealth

along the channels of stewardship and obedience. God looks for people who say, "Lord, I want more so that I can do more." People who see prosperity not as comfort, but as calling. When God blesses you, He is not rewarding you; He is recruiting you. He is saying, "Now that you have more, let's change more lives."

That is the heartbeat of divine abundance , not ownership, but partnership. God never blesses for isolation; He blesses for impact. He gives to the generous because He knows they will keep the river flowing. Heaven's abundance does not pool; it pours.

As I continued to meditate on that whisper from God, I realised that the Garden of Eden is not gone; it still lives as a spiritual picture of how life was meant to be. It represents the condition of a heart that walks in relationship with God, that trusts His provision, and that tends to what He has given. Every believer carries a garden within. Every dream, idea, skill, and passion is a seed waiting to be cultivated. But seeds do not grow in doubt; they grow in diligence.

Your calling might be your garden. Your work, your creativity, your relationships, your generosity , all of it is soil entrusted to you. God's command has never changed: Be fruitful. Fruitfulness is not automatic; it's intentional. You cannot reap what you refuse to tend. If you want to see increase, you must participate in the process. You must plant, water, and protect what God gives.

The truth is that every garden responds to attention. What you nurture grows. What you neglect withers. Your gifts are living things; your ideas are waiting for cultivation. God has already placed everything you need within reach, but He is waiting for you to activate it with action and faith. He provides the seed, but He expects the sower.

When I finally understood that, something settled in me. I stopped praying for abundance to appear and started thanking God for the abundance already available. I began to see His faithfulness not as something distant, but as something woven into my everyday life.

Divine Wealth

The sunrise was provision. The idea was provision. The opportunity was provision. And my responsibility was to recognise it, honour it, and multiply it.

That is the essence of God's blueprint for abundance. It is not about luck or timing or background. It is about alignment. When your spirit, mind, and actions align with God's principles, increase becomes inevitable. You don't have to chase what you were created to attract. Blessing naturally follows those who walk in faith, wisdom, and purpose.

Abundance is not a promise you hope for; it is a pattern you follow. It is the fruit of understanding that God is both your Provider and your Partner. You plant the seed; He sends the rain. You take the step; He makes the way. You obey the whisper; He multiplies the outcome. That is divine partnership.

So, wherever you are, take this to heart: you already have what you need to begin. The soil of your life is rich with potential. God has never called you to strive endlessly for what He has already placed within your reach. You were created in the image of an abundant God, and His blueprint for your life has always been fruitfulness. Your garden is waiting. The seeds are in your hands.

Trust the process. Cultivate what He has given you.

And watch how heaven responds.

Because when you live by God's blueprint, abundance doesn't just visit you , it becomes your atmosphere.

The more I began to study God's design for abundance, the more I realised how consistently He ties increase to purpose. In the Bible, every instance of wealth, growth, or multiplication was never random , it always served a divine assignment. God does not bless without reason; He blesses to reveal Himself. When you understand this, abundance stops being about accumulation and becomes about alignment.

Divine Wealth

Think about Joseph. He went from a pit to a palace, but not because he chased status. He simply walked faithfully in the blueprint of stewardship. Every time he was placed in a new environment, whether as a servant in Potiphar's house or a prisoner in Pharaoh's jail, Joseph didn't wait for better circumstances to be excellent. He cultivated excellence where he was. That's the mark of someone who understands divine design. Because the blueprint works in any environment, even in adversity.

When Pharaoh finally elevated Joseph, it wasn't wealth that changed him; it was wisdom that positioned him. He was trusted with the resources of a nation because he had first proven himself with the resources of a household. That is how God's economy works. You don't pray your way into abundance; you steward your way there. Jesus affirmed this in when He said, "Whoever can be trusted with very little can also be trusted with much." God measures faithfulness, not figures. Many people pray for overflow, but few prepare for it. They want the palace without learning to manage the prison. Yet God's blueprint always begins with stewardship.

That's why I believe the first law of abundance is The Law of Recognition. You cannot multiply what you do not recognise. God has already placed seeds of opportunity in your life, but if you don't see them, you can't sow them. Every gift, idea, connection, and skill is a seed waiting for your awareness. Recognition opens the door to revelation, and revelation leads to multiplication.

Moses recognised his staff. David recognised his sling. The widow recognised her small jar of oil. None of them had "enough" by human standards, but in the Kingdom, "enough" is whatever God blesses. The miracle is not in the size of what you hold; it's in the faith that holds it.

The second law is The Law of Stewardship. Once you recognise the seed, you must nurture it. Stewardship means treating what you have as sacred, not small. It means refusing to despise small beginnings

Divine Wealth

because you trust that everything great in the Kingdom starts small. The mustard seed was tiny, yet Jesus said it grows into a tree large enough for birds to nest in. Your business, your ministry, your creative gift, your influence , they are all seeds. God never hands anyone a tree; He gives a seed and watches how you plant it. Stewardship is not glamorous, but it's godly. It is the art of managing today with tomorrow in mind. It's budgeting your time, guarding your words, refining your skills, sowing consistently even when no one claps for you. The world calls that discipline. God calls it preparation.

The third law is The Law of Multiplication. Once you recognise and steward what God has given, He multiplies it through use. In Matthew 25, Jesus tells the parable of the talents. The servant who buried his gift in fear lost everything, but those who used their talents saw increase. The principle is simple but profound: what you bury dies; what you use grows. God never multiplies what we hide in fear. Too many believers are waiting for "more" before they begin, not realising that faith is the seed of increase. You don't wait for the harvest to sow; you sow because you believe the harvest will come. God blesses the bold. The moment you start acting on what He has placed in you, the divine flow begins.

And then there is The Law of Circulation. In the Kingdom, giving and receiving are not separate events; they are one continuous cycle. What you give creates space for what you're meant to receive. That's why the river flows, because it never hoards the water it carries. The Dead Sea is lifeless because it receives but never releases. Many Christians live like that sea , blessed, but stagnant. Yet God's design is not for you to be a reservoir; it's for you to be a river.

This is why Scripture says, "There is one who scatters, yet increases more, and there is one who withholds more than is right, but it leads to poverty." Heaven's logic runs opposite to the world's. What you

Divine Wealth

release, you retain in another form. What you hoard, you eventually lose. The hand that gives is never empty for long.

As I prayed through these principles, God began to show me that abundance is not something we wait for , it's something we grow into. It's the natural result of living in harmony with His laws. It's not a random miracle; it's the byproduct of alignment. When you live by the blueprint, you become predictable to heaven. God can trust you with more because He knows what you'll do with it.

But many of us struggle not because we lack resources, but because we have learned the wrong rhythm. We've been taught that hard work alone guarantees success. Yet countless people work hard without ever breaking through. Why? Because they work by the world's pattern, not God's. The world works for reward; the believer works from revelation. When you work from revelation, you understand that your effort is not the source , it's the seed.

Let me share something personal. When I first started applying these truths, I realised how much fear had quietly shaped my relationship with money. I would give, but always with a silent anxiety about what might come next. I'd plan for growth, but then talk myself out of it because I feared failing. And one day during prayer, God said, "You don't lack resources. You lack rest in Me." That sentence changed my life.

True abundance doesn't come from striving; it flows from surrender. When you trust God completely, you stop working for security and start working from peace. You understand that the same God who calls you to sow is the One who controls the rain. You plant faithfully, not fearfully.

That's why Jesus could sleep through storms. He wasn't indifferent; He was anchored. His rest was the ultimate proof of His trust. And that's the same rest you need to build from. You don't create abundance through worry; you create it through worship. You align your heart, your habits, and your hustle with heaven's rhythm.

Divine Wealth

The more I studied the Word, the more I saw how deeply God intertwines spiritual principles with practical ones. The book of Proverbs, often overlooked, is one of the greatest financial guides ever written. It teaches diligence, integrity, planning, generosity, and humility , all qualities of a wealthy soul. Solomon, the wisest and wealthiest man who ever lived, said, "Through wisdom a house is built, and by understanding it is established; by knowledge the rooms are filled with precious and pleasant riches."

Do you see it? Wisdom, understanding, and knowledge , these are the true building blocks of abundance. Not luck, not hustle, not shortcuts. God's blueprint begins in the mind before it manifests in the material. That's why the renewal of your thoughts is so critical. As long as you think like a struggler, you'll live like one, even when opportunity knocks. But when you begin to think like a steward, you prepare yourself for divine trust.

One of the most freeing truths I've learned is that God never calls us to wealth without also calling us to wisdom. Wealth without wisdom becomes waste. But when you pair prosperity with purpose, you create legacy. Godly abundance is not measured by what you keep; it's measured by what you contribute. When you give, invest, and serve from a pure heart, your wealth becomes a testimony, not a temptation.

In that sense, abundance is a mirror that reflects your maturity. It reveals what you value most. If you see wealth as power, it will control you. If you see wealth as purpose, it will empower you. The moment you understand that everything you have is borrowed from God for His mission, you stop clinging and start creating.

And here is a mystery I have come to love: generosity and growth are intertwined. You cannot grow in Christ without learning to give. Giving is the proof that greed has lost its grip on your soul. Every time you give, you break agreement with fear. You silence the

Divine Wealth

whisper that says, "What if there's not enough?" and replace it with faith that says, "God is more than enough."

That is the heartbeat of divine abundance , trust. The more you trust, the more you release. The more you release, the more God entrusts to you. It is a divine exchange, a rhythm of grace that transforms your entire life.

Now I understand why Jesus spoke more about money than almost any other subject. It wasn't because He was obsessed with it, but because He knew that how we handle money reveals how much we trust God. He said, "Where your treasure is, there your heart will be also." God doesn't need your money; He wants your heart. But He knows that your heart follows your habits. That's why your giving, saving, spending, and investing are all spiritual acts of worship.

When you live by God's blueprint, money stops being emotional chaos and becomes a tool for eternal purpose. You begin to budget by values, not pressure. You give intentionally, not impulsively. You build wealth not to boast, but to bless. You live open-handed, knowing that everything you release for God never truly leaves you , it just changes form.

That's the beauty of the Kingdom: nothing surrendered to God is ever lost. Every seed sown into His purpose returns multiplied. You may not always see it immediately, but divine timing always honours faithful stewardship. That's why reminds us, "Let us not grow weary in doing good, for in due season we shall reap, if we do not lose heart."

And when that harvest comes, it's never just material , it's spiritual, emotional, relational. You begin to walk in peace. You begin to think clearer. You begin to make decisions from vision, not from fear. Abundance becomes a mindset before it ever becomes a bank account.

I've come to believe that the greatest wealth God gives is wisdom. Because when wisdom leads, wealth follows. But when wealth leads,

Divine Wealth

wisdom fades. Wisdom shows you how to multiply without losing yourself. It teaches you how to enjoy abundance without being enslaved by it.

So, if you're reading this wondering where to start, start with what you already have. Your garden is not somewhere else , it's right where you are. The blueprint isn't distant , it's written in your spirit. God has already placed the pattern of increase within you. Your role is to recognise it, steward it, and trust Him to multiply it.

When you walk in that rhythm, you realise that prosperity is not pride , it's partnership. You are not chasing money; you are channelling purpose. You are not hoarding wealth; you are harvesting resources for Kingdom impact. You are not working for riches; you are working with revelation.

This is the divine blueprint: recognise the seed, steward it faithfully, multiply it through use, and keep the flow alive through generosity. This is how heaven's economy operates.

And when you live this way, abundance stops being a season and becomes your state. It becomes the way you move, think, and give. You no longer measure success by what you possess but by how many lives your obedience touches.

So today, take a deep breath and let this truth sink in: you were never meant to live in lack. The Author of life does not write stories of scarcity. His blueprint has always been fruitfulness. You were designed to flourish, to give, to build, to bless, and to reflect His abundance in every area of your life.

Lift your head and see your garden again. What has He placed in your hands? What has He whispered in your heart? What opportunities, however small, are waiting for your faith to activate them? Because that is where the blueprint begins , right there, in the ordinary places of obedience.

As you recognise it, tend it, and trust it, you will begin to see what I saw that Sunday morning. That abundance is not something you

Divine Wealth

chase; it's something you become. It's what happens when heaven and earth meet through a willing heart.

You are part of God's divine design. You are His chosen vessel of creation and multiplication. And if you follow His blueprint, your life will not only bear fruit , it will feed generations.

That is abundance God's way.

Divine Wealth

Chapter 2: Faith in Action: Stepping Into the Flow of Divine Provision

Divine Wealth

There comes a moment in every believer's journey when knowledge must turn into movement. You can know God's promises, quote His Word, even believe His goodness, but until faith turns into action, abundance remains potential, not reality. Understanding the blueprint is one thing, walking in it is another.

Faith is the bridge between revelation and manifestation. It is the invisible step that carries you from hearing God's Word to experiencing His provision. And yet, for many Christians, that bridge feels fragile. We pray for miracles but fear the first step. We say, "God, use me," but freeze when He opens the door. We want increase but hesitate when obedience demands motion.

But the truth is this, faith is not a feeling, it is a function. It moves even when the heart trembles. It obeys even when it cannot see. Faith is not the absence of uncertainty, it is the decision to trust God despite uncertainty.

When Peter stepped out of the boat to walk on water, he didn't wait for calm seas. He stepped in the middle of the storm. Faith rarely waits for comfort, it creates courage in discomfort. The sea beneath him didn't change until his feet moved. That is the nature of faith, the miracle begins at motion.

We often pray for God to part the waters before we move, but He is waiting for us to move before He parts the waters. The Jordan didn't open until the priests stepped in. The walls of Jericho didn't fall until Israel shouted. Provision doesn't flow to hesitation, it flows to obedience.

Faith activates divine provision, not because faith manipulates God, but because faith aligns us with His already-existing supply. Heaven's resources are not waiting to be created, they are waiting to be claimed. The warehouse of heaven is always full, faith is the key that opens its doors.

I have come to understand that faith is heaven's currency. It is not emotion, but exchange. Every time you trust God, you make a

Divine Wealth

spiritual transaction. You trade fear for favour, doubt for direction, comfort for calling. Faith is how we bank with heaven.

When you give, you are not losing, you are investing. When you obey, you are not surrendering power, you are unlocking it. When you trust God with what is in your hand, He entrusts you with what is in His. The problem is that many of us confuse believing in God with believing God. To believe in God is to acknowledge His existence, to believe God is to act as if His Word is true. The first requires agreement, the second requires action. The first moves your lips, the second moves your life.

Every major miracle in Scripture began with a command that didn't make sense. "Stretch out your hand." "Fill the jars with water." "Launch out into the deep." "Roll away the stone." "Go and wash in the pool." Faith always looks foolish until it works. But the Kingdom of God was never meant to make sense to the natural mind, it was meant to make miracles in obedient hearts.

This is the sacred paradox of faith, it feels risky, yet it is the safest place to be. Because faith is never about the size of the step, it is about the certainty of the Source.

When God tells you to give, start, sow, forgive, build, or speak, He is not testing your ability, He is training your trust. He already knows what's in you, He wants you to know what's in Him.

When you act in faith, something shifts in the spiritual realm. It is as if heaven inhales your obedience and exhales favour. Opportunities open, doors appear, ideas awaken. And though the world calls it luck, you know it's the pattern of grace.

Faith is not linear, it's relational. It doesn't follow logic, it follows love. The reason faith works is not because of what you believe, but because of Who you believe in. You can't manipulate God with faith, you cooperate with Him through it.

When Abraham left his home to follow God's call, he had no map. God didn't hand him coordinates, He handed him a promise. "Go to

Divine Wealth

the land I will show you." That one sentence defined his life. Faith rarely gives you the full picture, it gives you enough light for the next step. You move, then revelation moves with you.

Abraham's faith wasn't perfect. He doubted, he questioned, he made mistakes. But faith doesn't require perfection, it requires progression. God counts movement as trust. Even when you wobble, if your heart stays toward Him, you are still walking in faith.

One of the greatest lessons faith has taught me is that God doesn't bless hesitation. He blesses holy risk. Faith is not reckless, it is responsible courage. It doesn't ignore wisdom, it obeys wisdom even when wisdom looks wild. When the Spirit prompts you to start something, give something, or leave something, that prompting is not pressure, it's partnership. It's heaven's invitation to see what your obedience can unlock.

When Elijah told the widow of Zarephath to give her last meal, it seemed cruel. She was preparing to die. But Elijah wasn't taking from her, he was inviting her into the flow of divine provision. Her obedience turned scarcity into sustainability. What she thought was her last meal became her first miracle.

That story reveals something about the character of God. He never asks for what you can't give, He asks for what will grow your faith. And faith, once stretched, never shrinks back to its old size.

Faith not only opens heaven's supply, it transforms you. It rewires your thinking, expands your capacity, and sharpens your discernment. It turns ordinary people into divine conduits. That's why Scripture says, "The just shall live by faith." Faith is not a tool for crisis, it's a lifestyle for Kingdom living.

To live by faith means to walk daily in trust, not just occasionally in desperation. It means that your confidence is not in circumstances, but in covenant. You stop measuring your future by what's in your account and start measuring it by what's in God's Word.

Divine Wealth

This is where most believers wrestle. We want divine security while living with earthly control. But faith demands surrender. It asks you to loosen your grip and let God lead. It doesn't make you passive, it makes you powerful, because you're no longer striving in your own strength.

When you finally let go of the illusion of control, you discover the reality of flow. Flow is that sacred state where grace meets obedience, where effort becomes ease because alignment has replaced anxiety. Flow is not laziness, it is the divine rhythm of doing what God says, when He says, and how He says it.

Faith creates flow. It pulls you into motion with heaven. You begin to sense when to act, when to wait, when to sow, when to speak, when to rest. You stop forcing outcomes and start following instruction.

This is where miracles live, in the space between your obedience and God's outcome.

Faith is not the power to make God do something, it's the posture to let Him. It's agreement with His will even when you can't predict His ways. And every time you act in faith, you build spiritual momentum. Each small yes compounds into confidence. Each act of obedience trains your spirit to trust faster next time.

The world says, "I'll believe it when I see it." Faith says, "I'll see it when I believe it." The world measures risk by sight, faith measures it by revelation. And when you live by revelation, you see what others miss.

You begin to notice God's fingerprints in ordinary moments. The unexpected call, the new idea, the door that opens when you least expect it, these are not coincidences. They are confirmations. Faith sharpens your vision to recognise divine patterns where others see chance.

When you walk by faith, even detours become destiny. The delay you feared becomes development. The closed door becomes protection.

Divine Wealth

The loss becomes redirection. Nothing is wasted in the life of a believer who trusts God.
I've seen this truth unfold in my own life time and again. When I look back, every major blessing came wrapped in uncertainty. The moments I feared the most became the moments God proved Himself the most faithful. Faith didn't make life easier, it made it meaningful. It turned waiting into worship and trials into testimonies. You see, God's provision doesn't flow through striving, it flows through surrender. Faith is not about forcing doors open, it's about walking through the ones God unlocks. When you live this way, provision becomes natural. You stop chasing it because you realise you're standing in it.
The flow of divine provision is constant. It's like a river that never runs dry. The question is not whether it's flowing, the question is whether you are aligned with it. Faith is what positions you in the current. Fear steps out of it, faith stays in it.
And when you stay in the flow, something incredible happens, your life becomes effortless impact. Things that used to feel heavy become light. Situations that used to drain you now inspire you. You begin to work with heaven instead of against it.
That's what Jesus meant when He said, "My yoke is easy, and My burden is light." It wasn't that life would be without challenges, but that partnership with God changes the weight. Faith shifts your load from strain to strength.
Every time you act in faith, heaven moves closer. Every time you trust beyond reason, you give God room to reveal Himself. Every time you sow despite fear, you prove that your hope is not in what's in your hand, but in Who's holding your future.
Faith is heaven's favourite language. It's the sound of trust that echoes through eternity. And when God hears it, He responds.
Faith is more than a declaration, it is a direction. It is not a moment of passion at the altar, it is the quiet decision to keep trusting when

Divine Wealth

life feels uncertain. Real faith is not loud, it is loyal. It doesn't always shout, sometimes it simply stays.

There will be seasons when obedience feels invisible, when you pray and nothing seems to shift, when you sow and see no sprout, when you walk in faith but still face storms. In those moments, you will be tempted to question whether God sees you, whether heaven has heard your prayers. But those are the very moments when your faith is growing its roots.

Seeds do not shout while they are growing. They break in silence, beneath the soil, in the dark. So too does faith. What looks like delay is often development. God uses silence to strengthen your foundation, so that when your season of fruit comes, it can stand under the weight of blessing.

Do not confuse stillness with stagnation. Just because you can't see movement doesn't mean there isn't growth. The quiet seasons are not punishment, they are preparation. God does His best work beneath the surface.

Faith means trusting His process even when His pace feels slow. It means saying, "Lord, even if I can't see it, I still believe it." That single statement can shift your entire reality, because heaven responds to persistence.

When the woman with the issue of blood pressed through the crowd to touch Jesus' garment, she didn't wait for an invitation. She didn't wait for a perfect moment. She acted. Twelve years of pain could not silence her faith. She reached, and the moment her hand met His robe, her miracle met her need.

That is what faith does, it reaches. It pushes past what others call impossible. It refuses to let fear dictate the finish. Faith reaches for Jesus, even when logic says it won't work.

God is moved by movement. Every step of obedience you take sends a signal to heaven that says, "I trust You more than I trust what I see." And heaven always responds to trust.

Divine Wealth

Faith doesn't require certainty; it requires surrender. You don't need to know how it will work, you just need to know Who is working. When God told Noah to build an ark, there had never been rain. When He told Joshua to march around Jericho, the walls were thick and high. When He told Gideon to go into battle, his army was too small. None of it made sense, but obedience doesn't always need sense, it needs surrender.

Faith begins where logic ends. Logic looks for the numbers; faith listens for the voice.

If you wait until it makes sense, you'll miss the miracle. The miracle often hides in the instruction that feels strange. God will never ask you to do something that doesn't require trust, because trust is the proof of faith.

And when you follow that instruction, even trembling, you step into what I call the divine current. It's that sacred flow where grace begins to work for you instead of you trying to make everything work for yourself. It's where you start to notice divine timing, divine connections, divine opportunities. It's not coincidence; it's confirmation.

The divine current doesn't carry those who are idle, it carries those who move.

You cannot steer a still boat. God directs those who are in motion. That's why the Bible says, "Faith without works is dead." Faith must have form. Belief must have behaviour. What you believe internally must be expressed externally.

Sometimes that action looks like applying for the job, sometimes it looks like forgiving someone who hurt you, sometimes it looks like giving your last bit of savings to bless someone else. Sometimes faith looks like stillness, but that stillness is not passive; it's posture. It's the posture of someone waiting in trust, not in fear.

Faith is not always about leaping; sometimes it's about lasting. It is the consistency of trust that transforms the heart.

Divine Wealth

Every step of faith becomes a seed. You may not see the harvest immediately, but heaven never forgets a seed. Every act of obedience is recorded, every tear of surrender is noticed, every "yes" whispered in private echoes loudly in heaven.

You will find that faith's fruit often appears in unexpected ways. God might not answer in the way you imagined, but He will always answer in the way that transforms you. Sometimes He gives you what you ask for, sometimes He gives you what you truly need. And in both, He is good.

The truth is, you will not always feel faith; you will have to choose it. Feelings fluctuate, faith remains. Faith is not sustained by emotion but by conviction. When doubt knocks, faith answers with remembrance. It reminds you of every storm you've survived, every mountain that moved, every closed door that led to something better. Faith grows through memory. That's why testimonies matter. Every time you recall what God has done before, you strengthen your spirit for what He will do next. The same God who parted the Red Sea is the same God who will part the obstacles before you. The same God who fed Elijah with ravens is the same God who will feed you in famine. The same God who provided manna in the wilderness can still make a way in your dry season.

He hasn't changed. His nature is still faithful, His hand is still generous, His plan is still perfect. The only question is whether you will keep walking when the path feels unfamiliar.

Faith doesn't ask for evidence, it creates it. When you step forward, even trembling, heaven confirms your courage. The evidence comes after the act, not before it.

That's why Scripture says, "Now faith is the substance of things hoped for, the evidence of things not seen." Faith is the substance before the sight. It is the invisible confidence that builds visible results.

Divine Wealth

When God calls you to move, He is not setting you up for failure; He is setting you up for formation. Faith forms your character before it fulfills your calling. The promise is never the first step; preparation is. God often hides His promises behind obedience. He tells you to move, give, or trust, not because He needs what's in your hand, but because He's preparing your heart. The test is never about the thing; it's about the trust.

And if you can trust Him in the small things, you'll be ready when He gives you big things.

I remember a time when I was standing at a crossroads in my life, unsure which direction to take. I prayed, fasted, and sought counsel, but heaven felt quiet. It was only when I decided to move in faith, trusting that God would correct me if I was wrong, that peace flooded my heart. It wasn't that God had been silent; He was simply waiting for movement.

That moment taught me something profound , faith doesn't eliminate fear; it overrides it. Courage is not the absence of fear, it's obedience in the presence of it.

You can walk on water and still feel the wind. You can step into the unknown and still feel uncertain. But if you keep your eyes on Jesus, you won't sink; you'll soar.

The key is focus. Faith fixes its gaze on God, not the waves. When Peter began to sink, it wasn't because the storm grew stronger, it was because his attention shifted. He took his eyes off Jesus and looked at the wind.

Faith grows where focus stays. Whatever you magnify becomes your master. If you focus on problems, they expand. If you focus on promises, peace expands. Faith feeds on focus.

And focus grows through gratitude. Gratitude is the language of faith. When you thank God in advance, you are telling heaven, "I trust You to finish what You started." Gratitude turns waiting into

Divine Wealth

worship. It transforms delay into dialogue. It keeps your heart open and your hope alive.

The flow of divine provision is always available, but it requires a grateful posture. Gratitude guards your perspective when outcomes take time. It reminds you that God has already done enough to deserve your trust.

If you want to stay in the flow of faith, keep your heart soft, your hands open, and your words aligned with God's promises. Speak faith even when fear whispers otherwise. Declare His truth over your circumstances. Faith is not silent; it speaks life.

Every "I believe" you speak becomes an anchor in the spirit. Every "It is well" becomes a declaration that shifts the atmosphere. Heaven responds to words spoken in faith. The universe itself was formed by a spoken word, and that same creative power lives in you.

You are made in the image of a speaking God. When you speak in faith, you echo His authority. That is how mountains move. They respond to voices anchored in belief.

So speak the Word, not your worry. Speak the promise, not the problem. Speak faith, even when your feelings say otherwise. Because faith is not about pretending everything is fine; it's about proclaiming that God is faithful, even when it's not.

And the moment you do, the atmosphere shifts. Hope returns. Peace fills the room. You begin to feel heaven breathing through your words.

Faith turns waiting rooms into worship spaces. It transforms "not yet" into "soon."

When you start to live this way, something changes inside you. You no longer chase outcomes; you chase obedience. You no longer live for applause; you live for alignment. You stop measuring life by what happens to you and start measuring it by what flows through you. That's when you truly step into the divine flow.

Divine Wealth

The divine flow is not about everything going right; it's about everything working for good. It's the awareness that even in detours, God is directing. Even in delay, God is developing. Even in difficulty, God is deepening your faith.

And when you live in that awareness, nothing can shake your peace. Because you know that the same God who parted the Red Sea can part your obstacles, the same God who sent manna can meet your needs, and the same God who raised Lazarus can resurrect your dreams.

That is faith in action. It's not just believing for blessings; it's becoming the kind of person who walks so closely with God that blessings can't help but follow.

Faith turns believers into builders. It turns prayers into plans. It turns dreams into divine demonstrations. Faith is what bridges your calling to your completion.

And the most beautiful thing about it all is that God never leaves you to do it alone. Every time you step out in faith, He steps with you. Every time you obey, His hand covers you. Every time you trust, His grace strengthens you.

You were never meant to walk by sight, you were designed to walk by trust. You were never meant to chase provision, you were meant to walk with the Provider. You were never meant to build alone, you were meant to build with heaven.

When you finally realise that, peace will flood your heart. You will stop striving and start flowing. You will stop trying to prove and start producing. You will stop worrying about outcomes and start worshipping through them.

Because when faith is in motion, heaven is too.

And that, beloved, is what it means to live in the flow of divine provision , to move with God in trust, to speak His promises in hope, and to see your life become a living testimony of what happens when faith meets obedience.

Divine Wealth

That is the rhythm of the Kingdom, that is the power of faith in action, and that is the invitation waiting before you now.
Step in, the river is already flowing.

Divine Wealth

Chapter 3: The Power of Stewardship: Multiplying What God Has Placed in Your Hands

Divine Wealth

Everything God gives carries potential. Nothing He places in your hands is empty, and nothing He entrusts to you is ordinary. The challenge is not whether He has given, but whether you can see what He has given. Every blessing, every opportunity, every skill, and every idea is a seed designed to multiply when placed in faithful hands. Stewardship is the bridge between God's provision and His promise. It is the quiet art of managing well what heaven entrusts to you. Many people pray for more, but few prepare for it. God doesn't withhold blessings, He withholds premature burdens. He waits until He sees maturity in our management before multiplying what we hold.

Stewardship is not simply about money, it is about mentality. It is a mindset that says, "I may not have everything I want, but I will be faithful with everything I have." It is the attitude that transforms little into much, and ordinary into extraordinary. God never blesses waste, but He always multiplies wisdom.

When Jesus told the parable of the talents in Matthew 25, He revealed a divine pattern. The master gave his servants different measures of resources, not as a test of equality, but of responsibility. Each servant received something, and each had the opportunity to multiply it. The two who invested and increased what they were given heard the words every believer longs for: "Well done, good and faithful servant." The one who buried his gift out of fear, however, lost even what he had.

That story is not just about ancient servants, it is about us. God has placed something within each of us that He expects to grow. The tragedy of burying potential is that it silences purpose. You may think you're playing it safe, but in the Kingdom, safety without faith becomes stagnation.

Stewardship requires trust, but it also requires vision. Vision is the ability to see beyond what is into what could be. When you look at

Divine Wealth

what God has placed in your hands, don't just see what it is, see what it can become when blessed, refined, and multiplied.

A single seed can produce an orchard if you nurture it. The difference between the barren and the fruitful is not God's generosity, but our stewardship. One person looks at a small beginning and says, "This is not enough," while another looks at the same beginning and says, "This is the start of something greater."

The heart of stewardship begins with gratitude. You cannot multiply what you do not value. Gratitude shifts your perspective from lack to abundance. When you thank God for what's in your hand, you acknowledge its divine origin. Gratitude is not a small habit, it's a spiritual key. It unlocks contentment, opens creativity, and invites multiplication.

Jesus demonstrated this when He fed the five thousand. He didn't complain about the small number of loaves and fish, He lifted them and gave thanks. Gratitude preceded the miracle. Before the bread multiplied, thanksgiving multiplied. The miracle began not in His hands, but in His heart.

Many believers wait for more before they start giving thanks, but heaven waits for thanks before it releases more. Gratitude is the signal that says, "I trust You, God, even when it looks small." And when God finds a grateful steward, He pours out blessings that overflow.

Stewardship also means accountability. It means living with the awareness that what you have is not yours to own, but yours to manage. Ownership says, "This belongs to me." Stewardship says, "This belongs to God, and I am its guardian." That single shift changes everything.

When you live as an owner, you carry the weight of control. When you live as a steward, you carry the peace of trust. You understand that the pressure to provide is not yours, the responsibility to be faithful is. God never asked you to perform miracles, He asked you

Divine Wealth

to manage faithfully. He performs the multiplication, you manage the moment.

Stewardship is sacred partnership. It is heaven saying, "I'll provide the resources if you provide the responsibility."

Think of Joseph in Egypt. He wasn't born into wealth or power. He was betrayed, enslaved, and imprisoned. Yet, wherever he was placed, he managed with excellence. In Potiphar's house, he became the head servant. In prison, he became the warden's assistant. And when Pharaoh needed someone to oversee an entire nation's economy, God elevated Joseph to second-in-command. Why? Because Joseph had already proven himself a faithful steward in smaller systems.

Stewardship prepares you for promotion. Promotion is not a miracle, it is a measurement of management. Heaven observes how you handle what you already have before entrusting you with what's next. That's why Scripture says, "He who is faithful in little will be faithful in much."

We often pray for more resources, but God is watching how we handle the ones we already possess. Are we disciplined? Are we generous? Are we diligent? Are we grateful? The answers to these questions determine whether heaven increases our supply.

Stewardship is not just financial, it touches every area of life. It is how you manage your time, your relationships, your health, your calling, your emotions, and your influence. Everything you have been given is an assignment wrapped in opportunity.

When you treat your time as holy, you multiply impact. When you treat your body as a temple, you multiply energy. When you treat relationships as divine connections, you multiply trust. When you treat your calling as sacred, you multiply fruitfulness.

Excellence is a form of worship. Doing your best with what you have is how you honour the One who gave it. The world may never notice your discipline, but heaven does. God sees every quiet act of

Divine Wealth

faithfulness, the extra effort, the unseen kindness, the diligent preparation. These are the seeds that heaven waters.

Stewardship is love in action. It says, "God, I trust You enough to take care of what You've entrusted to me." It's how faith turns into form. You can't say you trust God to give increase if you neglect what you already hold. Increase is not magic, it's momentum built through consistency.

God is not looking for perfect people, He is looking for faithful ones. Perfection exhausts, faithfulness multiplies. You may not have the best start, but faithfulness guarantees a strong finish. God honours consistency more than charisma.

When you wake up each morning and decide to keep showing up, keep giving, keep believing, you are planting seeds that will one day grow into testimonies. You may not see the fruit yet, but heaven is watching your faithfulness. The same God who counts the stars counts your efforts.

Stewardship also requires wisdom. Faith without wisdom leads to frustration. Wisdom shows you how to handle the blessings God sends. Without it, abundance can become a burden. The same blessing that was meant to elevate you can overwhelm you if you mismanage it.

Wisdom is the compass of stewardship. It teaches you to plan, to budget, to save, to give, and to invest with discernment. The book of Proverbs says, "By wisdom a house is built, and by understanding it is established." If faith opens the door, wisdom builds the foundation.

To steward well is to listen well. Every resource you have carries divine instruction. God does not give randomly, He gives intentionally. He hides wisdom inside your blessings. If you listen closely, your resources will tell you how to multiply them.

Money will whisper, "Manage me." Time will whisper, "Prioritise me." Gifts will whisper, "Develop me." Relationships will whisper,

Divine Wealth

"Protect me." Your body will whisper, "Rest me." Every area of your life speaks, but only the wise steward listens.

If you ignore the whispers of stewardship, you eventually hear the noise of lack. But if you honour the small instructions, you begin to experience peace, order, and growth.

There is something profoundly spiritual about organisation. Heaven moves in order. Creation itself began with structure, light separated from darkness, waters divided, seasons appointed. Order precedes abundance. If you bring order to what you have, God brings overflow to what you touch.

Stewardship turns chaos into clarity. It invites divine flow into every area of your life. When your finances are in order, you feel lighter. When your time is managed well, you feel purposeful. When your priorities are aligned, your peace returns.

Many people pray for miracles when what they truly need is management. Miracles happen in moments, but stewardship sustains them. God can bless you today, but without stewardship, tomorrow you'll lose what you gained. That's why wisdom is wealth's greatest companion.

True prosperity is not having more, it's managing better. God doesn't measure success by accumulation, but by administration. What matters most is not how much passes through your hands, but how faithfully you handle it.

There is a quiet power in being intentional. When you treat your work, your home, your giving, and your calling with purpose, you honour God's character. He is not careless, and you were made in His image. His order runs through your spirit, and His excellence lives within your design.

Stewardship is not bondage, it's freedom. When you learn to manage, you break the chains of chaos. You stop being reactive and start being proactive. You move from scarcity thinking to stewardship

Divine Wealth

thinking, from "I don't have enough" to "I have more than enough to begin."

The enemy's greatest deception is to make you believe that small means insignificant. But every great move of God began with something small. David's stone, Moses' staff, Elijah's jar of oil, Jesus' loaves and fish, all small, all powerful.

The difference was stewardship. Each was placed in the hands of someone who saw divine potential in simplicity. You don't need to wait for something big to begin, you need to begin with something small.

Stewardship sees hidden potential. It looks at the seed and envisions the harvest. It looks at today's little and sees tomorrow's legacy. It believes that God's increase always begins with faithfulness in the ordinary.

When you steward with love and diligence, heaven begins to trust you with more. The principle of divine trust is clear, God will not give you what you cannot handle. But when you prove faithful, He expands your capacity.

That is why promotion in the Kingdom is not a reward, it's a responsibility. The more God gives you, the more people He intends to bless through you. You become a distribution channel for His goodness.

Stewardship transforms success into service. It takes wealth out of selfishness and returns it to worship. The goal is not to gather riches, but to become rich in purpose, rich in wisdom, rich in giving, rich in love.

When you live as a steward, you stop chasing money and start attracting meaning. You stop asking for more and start asking for wisdom. You realise that the greatest wealth is the ability to manage well the gifts God has already placed in your care.

Divine Wealth

And when you do, everything you touch begins to multiply, not because you're striving, but because you're aligned. You are living in rhythm with heaven's order.

Every blessing God gives is a trust, and every trust is a test. What you do with what He places in your hands reveals what He can place in your future. The more I have learned about the nature of God, the more I see that He doesn't measure wealth by what we hold, but by what we handle well. Heaven is not impressed by accumulation; heaven is moved by administration.

Stewardship is not about how much you possess, but how you position what you possess for purpose. When you align your resources with God's will, you step into divine multiplication. Multiplication is not an accident of arithmetic; it is a law of heaven that responds to faithfulness. The same way gravity pulls objects toward the earth, stewardship pulls blessings toward your life.

The first law of multiplication is the law of release. Nothing multiplies while it is clutched too tightly. What you hold with fear cannot grow. What you release with faith cannot fail. The boy with the five loaves and two fish didn't have enough to feed a multitude, but when he released it to Jesus, what was insufficient became abundant. God cannot bless what you will not release. The open hand becomes the fertile ground of heaven.

You may think your gift is small, your time limited, your capacity ordinary, but in the hands of God, small becomes supernatural. The widow's oil didn't multiply until she started pouring. The jars didn't fill until she lifted them. That is how heaven works. You move first, then God multiplies. You act in faith, then He adds in favour.

The second law of multiplication is the law of refinement. Everything God entrusts to you must pass through the fire of faithfulness before it can be enlarged. Just as gold must be purified to reveal its true brilliance, your gifts, dreams, and opportunities must be refined through consistency, humility, and obedience. God will never

Divine Wealth

promote what pride would destroy. The fire does not come to burn you; it comes to build you.

Refinement teaches us discipline, patience, and perspective. You begin to understand that success without stewardship is dangerous. A blessing mismanaged becomes a burden. That is why God trains you before He trusts you. He allows seasons of testing not to punish you, but to prepare you. Every delay in the Kingdom carries design. God waits until the foundation of your character can carry the weight of His blessing.

The third law of multiplication is the law of purpose. God multiplies only what aligns with His will. He is not obligated to increase what exists outside His design. Many chase wealth for their own comfort, but divine wealth is assigned to divine cause. When your purpose is pure, your provision is secure. Money without mission becomes meaningless. But when wealth flows toward purpose, it becomes worship.

Stewardship, at its core, is worship. It is not what you give; it is how you give. It is not what you build; it is why you build. Every decision you make about your resources is an act of honour or an act of fear. Worship is not confined to song; it is expressed in management. How you handle what you have is the truest reflection of what you believe about God.

If you believe He is generous, you will give freely. If you believe He is faithful, you will plan wisely. If you believe He is Lord, you will manage humbly. The way you steward reveals the way you see Him. A faithful steward sees God not as a distant deity, but as an active partner in every detail of life.

When you make stewardship worship, your ordinary actions become sacred. Budgeting becomes prayer. Saving becomes vision. Giving becomes declaration. Serving becomes devotion. You begin to live every moment as an offering.

Divine Wealth

True stewardship says, "Everything I have belongs to God, and I am honoured to use it in His name." That mindset removes pride and plants peace. You no longer compete with others, because you realise that your assignment is unique. Comparison dies in the presence of purpose.

When you live as a steward, you also learn the law of circulation. Nothing God gives is meant to stay stagnant. Heaven's economy flows like a river. The blessing comes to you so it can move through you. When you give, you make space for more. When you hoard, you halt the flow.

Proverbs says, "There is one who gives freely, yet grows richer, and another who withholds more than is right, but it leads to poverty." That verse is a divine paradox that only faith can understand. In the Kingdom, release equals increase. When your giving flows, so does your growth.

God's abundance is not random; it follows rhythm. Seedtime and harvest, sowing and reaping, giving and receiving,this is the heartbeat of heaven. To break the flow of generosity is to step out of divine rhythm. You cannot outgive God. Every seed sown in faith returns as multiplied favour. It may not return in the same form, but it always returns in God's perfect timing.

When you become a vessel of giving, you become a vessel God trusts to fill. He looks for hearts that understand that blessings are meant to move. You are not the endpoint of His goodness; you are the extension of it.

Stewardship teaches you that increase is never for self-glory; it is for kingdom glory. When your hands stay open, your heart stays pure. You begin to see that wealth is not the destination; it is the tool. Money becomes ministry. Business becomes blessing. Influence becomes intercession.

When you realise that your success is a platform for service, your whole life begins to shift. You start asking, "How can I use what I

Divine Wealth

have to lift someone else?" That is when true abundance begins. You stop chasing recognition and start pursuing responsibility. You stop striving for approval and start seeking impact.

The heart of stewardship beats for contribution. The more you grow, the more you give. The more you give, the more you become.

Because in God's economy, giving does not diminish you; it develops you.

I have come to believe that giving is the highest expression of stewardship. It is the evidence that money does not master you. It is the language of freedom. Every time you give, you declare that God is your source, not your salary. You remind yourself that you are a vessel, not a vault.

Stewardship calls us to generosity not as a reaction, but as a rhythm. Generosity should not depend on emotion; it should be a lifestyle. The mature steward gives before the need appears, because giving is no longer a sacrifice; it is a joy.

Scripture says, "God loves a cheerful giver." The word "cheerful" in Greek is "hilaros," from which we get "hilarious." Imagine that, God loves a giver who laughs while giving, a soul so free from fear that joy erupts in generosity. That is what stewardship produces, the freedom to give with delight.

To live in that level of faith, you must learn the law of contentment. Contentment is not complacency; it is confidence in God's provision. It means knowing that your worth is not defined by what you own, but by Whose you are. A content heart can handle increase, because it doesn't depend on it.

When Paul wrote, "I have learned to be content in every situation," he was writing from prison. Yet even in lack, he spoke of abundance. Contentment does not mean settling for less; it means being secure in God's timing. It is knowing that whether you are in a season of plenty or pruning, God is still good, and His plan is still perfect.

Divine Wealth

Contentment creates capacity. When your heart is at rest, your hands are free to receive. Anxiety clutters your soul, but peace makes space for provision. Stewardship is sustained by peace. You cannot manage what you constantly fear losing. The steward who trusts in God's faithfulness finds rest even in responsibility.

As your faith matures, you begin to understand that stewardship is not seasonal; it is eternal. It doesn't end when life is comfortable, and it doesn't crumble when life is difficult. True stewardship outlives circumstance. It becomes character.

Your stewardship today shapes your legacy tomorrow. Everything you manage well multiplies beyond your lifetime. The wisdom you apply, the generosity you model, the integrity you maintain,these become seeds that outlive you. The next generation will eat fruit from the trees you plant today.

This is the mystery of divine stewardship,it creates continuity. It connects heaven to earth, present to future, you to eternity. Every act of faithfulness adds to a legacy of light that no darkness can erase. When you manage your resources with purpose, heaven records your stewardship as worship. The world measures success by what you accumulate; heaven measures it by what you distribute. You are not called to die rich; you are called to live poured out.

One day, each of us will stand before God, and He will not ask, "How much did you make?" He will ask, "How much did you multiply for My Kingdom?" And in that moment, what will matter most is not the size of your bank account, but the size of your obedience.

The reward for stewardship is not just eternal; it is experiential. When you live as a faithful steward, you begin to taste heaven on earth. Peace fills your home. Purpose fills your heart. Joy fills your days. You live lighter, freer, and fuller.

God begins to trust you with opportunities that others overlook. Doors open that no man can shut. Resources flow from unexpected

Divine Wealth

places. It is as if the universe itself conspires to support your calling, because you have become a trustworthy vessel of divine purpose. Stewardship is the key that turns management into miracles. It transforms the natural into the supernatural. When you bring order, God brings overflow. When you align your heart, heaven releases abundance.

And so I say this to you, never underestimate what God can do through a faithful steward. You may feel unseen, you may feel small, but heaven is watching your diligence. Every act of excellence is noticed. Every faithful choice is recorded. Every seed of obedience is counted.

Your faithfulness will speak for you when your words cannot. Your diligence will defend you when others doubt you. Your stewardship will open doors that talent alone never could.

If you stay faithful, what is in your hands today will become what changes lives tomorrow. You are the vessel God has chosen to multiply His goodness in the world. Your job is not to question how; your job is to stay faithful with the now.

For everything begins with stewardship. Faith opens the door, stewardship keeps it open. Faith attracts the promise, stewardship protects it. Faith starts the journey, stewardship sustains it.

And when your story is written, heaven will not measure your greatness by what you gathered, but by what you gave.

Be the steward who multiplies. Be the servant who manages with joy. Be the believer who turns every resource into revelation. For that is the power of stewardship,to take what is temporary and turn it into something eternal.

And as you do, remember this simple truth: God will always do more with your little than you could ever do with your much.

So hold loosely, manage wisely, give freely, and trust deeply. For the One who gave you the seed is also the One who controls the harvest.

Divine Wealth

And when He finds you faithful, He will fill your hands again and again, until your life overflows with purpose, peace, and praise.
That is the miracle of stewardship, and that is how you multiply what God has placed in your hands.

Divine Wealth

Chapter 4: The Kingdom Law of Increase: How God Expands What You Believe For

Divine Wealth

Increase is not an accident, it is an atmosphere. It surrounds those who expect it, it follows those who prepare for it, and it manifests for those who believe for it. The Kingdom of God operates on the law of faith, and faith, when acted upon, always produces increase. Everything God touches multiplies. His nature is abundance, and His intention for your life is expansion.

The first command He ever gave humanity was not about survival, it was about fruitfulness. "Be fruitful and multiply." These words were not just biological, they were spiritual. They were a declaration of identity, a divine instruction that flows through the very DNA of creation. God designed the universe to respond to growth, not stagnation. Everything living was created to reproduce, to expand, to overflow.

When God created the world, He didn't stop at sufficiency, He created abundance. He filled the skies with stars beyond counting, the oceans with fish beyond measure, the earth with seeds beyond imagination. He did not create scarcity, He created supply. Scarcity entered the world through fear and disobedience, not through design. That is why living in increase is not greed, it is alignment. You were not meant to live in perpetual lack, you were meant to live in divine flow. The problem is not that God has stopped providing, it's that many have stopped believing. Faith is the bridge between divine intention and human experience.

Increase begins with belief. What you believe sets the boundaries for what you receive. You cannot live beyond the limits of your faith. Scripture says, "According to your faith, let it be done to you." Heaven does not move according to emotion, it moves according to expectation.

If you expect small, you experience small. If you expect abundance, you attract abundance. Not because God loves one person more than another, but because faith creates capacity. Faith stretches your spirit to receive what God already desires to give.

Divine Wealth

That is the Kingdom law of increase, God will only fill what you make room for.

When the widow came to Elisha in desperation, her husband gone and her sons threatened with slavery, she had nothing but a small jar of oil. Elisha told her to borrow as many vessels as she could and start pouring. The oil only stopped flowing when the jars stopped coming. The supply ended where the capacity ended. The miracle did not depend on God's willingness, it depended on her preparation. God has already released everything you will ever need into the atmosphere of faith. But the measure you receive is determined by the space you create. Empty jars represent expectancy. They are symbols of faith saying, "God, I'm ready for more."

Increase is not just a financial concept, it is a spiritual principle. It is about enlarging your capacity to love, to forgive, to serve, to give, to create, and to believe. The law of increase applies to every area of your life because everything in the Kingdom is designed to grow. Jesus said the Kingdom of heaven is like a mustard seed. It starts small, almost invisible, but when it grows, it becomes a tree large enough for birds to rest in its branches. The seed does not stay small because it was never meant to. Small beginnings are not signs of insignificance, they are invitations to faith.

Do not despise your beginnings. God never starts big, He starts right. He plants potential, not perfection. The miracle is not in the size of your start, but in the soil of your stewardship. When you nurture what God gives you, He breathes increase into it.

The law of increase teaches us that God multiplies movement, not stagnation. He blesses the doer, not the dreamer. You can pray for abundance, but until you plant something, heaven has nothing to multiply. Prayer opens the heavens, action opens the harvest.

God cannot increase what you refuse to initiate. The seed that stays in your pocket will never feed the multitude. The dream that stays in

Divine Wealth

your mind will never impact the world. The idea that never leaves your journal will never change a life.

Increase begins when you take what is in your hand and use it in faith. Every time you sow effort, obedience, love, or generosity, you activate divine multiplication. The act of release creates the atmosphere of return.

The reason many never experience increase is because they confuse waiting with watching. Waiting on God is not passive observation, it is active preparation. To wait on God is to ready your field for rain. It is to build your barn before the harvest comes. It is to live in expectation, not in hesitation.

Faith does not wait for confirmation, it creates it. It moves as if the miracle is already in motion.

When you begin to walk in this revelation, you realise that God is not withholding your blessing, He is watching your readiness. Increase is not about convincing God, it's about aligning with Him. He is always willing to expand you, but He will not expand you beyond your maturity.

The law of increase demands growth in both faith and responsibility. It requires you to think bigger, believe deeper, and act wiser. If your mindset remains small, your miracle remains distant. That is why renewal of the mind is central to the life of faith. The spirit of increase cannot dwell in a heart of limitation.

Renew your vision daily. Refuse to shrink your dreams to fit your comfort. God is always stretching those He intends to enlarge. The discomfort you feel is not punishment, it is preparation. Growth always costs comfort. The seed must break to become fruitful.

So when God allows pressure, it is because He sees potential. He stretches you because He knows what's inside you. He prunes your life not to reduce you, but to refine you. The branch that bears fruit is pruned to bear even more.

Divine Wealth

Do not fear divine pruning. Every cut carries promise. Every loss hides a lesson. Every delay carries destiny. God prunes what He plans to promote.

The Kingdom law of increase also reveals something extraordinary about timing. Growth happens in seasons. There are moments to plant, moments to water, moments to wait, and moments to harvest. Understanding seasons keeps your faith from frustration.

Many believers lose hope not because God denied their request, but because they misread their season. A seed planted in spring will not bear fruit in winter. Timing is God's invisible hand guiding your increase. He makes all things beautiful in their time, not before, not after.

Your job is not to force fruit, it is to stay faithful in your field. Keep tending your soil, keep watering your seed, keep believing in the unseen. The moment you stop nurturing what God gave, you stop inviting increase.

There will always be moments when progress feels invisible. That's because growth often happens underground. The seed germinates in silence before it grows in sight. Just because you can't see change doesn't mean God isn't working. The unseen is where increase begins.

That is why faith must see beyond the visible. The farmer doesn't question the soil every day, he trusts the process. Likewise, you must trust the promise even when the field looks empty. The same God who planted the seed will send the rain.

Increase requires trust in divine timing and trust in divine transformation. The waiting season is not wasted, it is woven with wisdom. God grows your patience before He grows your platform. He expands your character before He expands your calling.

The law of increase operates on stewardship, faith, and persistence. Stewardship keeps what you have in order, faith invites what you do

Divine Wealth

not yet have, and persistence keeps you believing between the two. Increase is not for the impatient, it is for the intentional.

Every time you choose discipline over distraction, you sow into increase. Every time you choose generosity over greed, you prepare for overflow. Every time you choose faith over fear, you expand your spiritual territory.

The law of increase is not random, it is relational. It flows through your connection with God. As you draw closer to Him, you align yourself with His abundance. You begin to see that increase is not separate from intimacy, it is born from it.

God doesn't just want to bless your hands, He wants to expand your heart. He doesn't just want to fill your storehouse, He wants to fill your spirit. True increase begins in your inner life. When peace grows, provision follows. When gratitude expands, generosity flows. When love deepens, opportunities open.

Increase is holistic. It touches your soul before it touches your surroundings. You cannot experience external growth without internal grace. That is why the law of increase begins not with what you have, but with what you believe.

You must believe that God desires your increase, not your limitation. You must believe that He takes pleasure in your prosperity. You must believe that His plan for you includes expansion, excellence, and elevation.

He said in Jeremiah, "For I know the plans I have for you, plans to prosper you and not to harm you, plans to give you a future and a hope." Prosperity is not a dirty word when it is pursued with pure motives. It simply means to flourish, to thrive, to advance toward your purpose.

When your heart is anchored in humility and your motive is anchored in ministry, increase becomes holy. You no longer chase wealth, you chase worthiness. You no longer desire possessions, you desire purpose. And as you do, abundance follows.

Divine Wealth

God increases those who increase others. When your vision includes blessing others, heaven invests in you. The Kingdom law of increase is reciprocal, what you make happen for others, God makes happen for you.

Every time you sow encouragement, you reap joy. Every time you give opportunity, you receive favour. Every time you extend grace, you attract mercy. That is divine economics, a system that multiplies goodness by giving it away.

And so, as you step into this revelation, remember that increase is not a destination, it is a dynamic relationship with God. It is the daily decision to believe that He can and will do exceedingly, abundantly, above all you ask or imagine.

Your belief sets the boundary for your blessing. If you can believe it, God can perform it.

The Kingdom law of increase begins with a whisper in your heart, a holy discontent that says, "There must be more." That whisper is not greed, it is grace inviting you to grow. God stirs that desire not to overwhelm you, but to awaken you.

The desire for more is not sinful when it is surrendered. It becomes sinful only when it replaces surrender. So desire boldly, but desire through God's lens. Ask for more wisdom, more compassion, more creativity, more influence, more opportunity, not for self-exaltation, but for Kingdom expansion.

For when your motive aligns with His mission, nothing can stop your increase.

Increase is not only a principle of heaven; it is the heartbeat of creation. Everything around you bears witness to the divine rhythm of multiplication. The trees that drop their seeds, the rivers that carve their paths, the stars that continue to burn and birth light into eternity , all creation testifies to one truth: growth is God's signature. To resist growth is to resist grace, because increase is not the reward of effort alone, it is the response to alignment.

Divine Wealth

When you live in alignment with God's purpose, you live under open heaven. The atmosphere around you begins to cooperate with His will. What was once delayed begins to accelerate. What was once difficult begins to flow. Divine increase is not something you chase; it is something you attract by becoming the person who can sustain it. The law of increase is not about getting more; it is about becoming more. Before God can increase what is in your hand, He increases what is in your heart. Abundance flows through transformation. The more you grow in faith, humility, and wisdom, the greater your capacity to carry the weight of His blessing.

There is a reason why Jesus taught through parables about seeds, soil, and growth. He understood that the human heart mirrors the earth. It must be prepared, tilled, and tended for increase to take root. The condition of your heart determines the fruit of your harvest.

A heart hardened by fear cannot receive the seed of faith. A heart cluttered by greed cannot host the seed of grace. But a heart surrendered in trust, filled with gratitude and guided by love, becomes fertile ground for miracles.

Increase begins in the invisible, long before it becomes visible. It starts with how you think, what you speak, and how you believe. Words shape worlds. Faith-filled words prepare the soil of your spirit for the seeds of destiny. When you speak life over your finances, over your purpose, over your future, you align your atmosphere with heaven's intent.

The enemy understands this principle well, which is why he tries to plant doubt before faith can take root. He whispers, "You'll never have enough, you're not worthy, others are chosen but not you." These lies are designed to shrink your expectation and silence your seed. But when you counter lies with truth, you reclaim your authority.

Scripture says, "Life and death are in the power of the tongue." This is not poetic exaggeration; it is a spiritual law. Every declaration you

Divine Wealth

make either multiplies faith or magnifies fear. Speak increase even when you feel surrounded by decrease. Declare God's promises even when your circumstances contradict them. Faith does not deny reality, it defies limitation.

You serve a God who called things that were not as though they were. The moment He spoke light, darkness had to flee. When you speak with faith, you echo the voice of creation itself. That is why the believer's language must always carry the sound of increase.

Increase also requires partnership. God rarely releases abundance to isolation. He works through relationships, collaborations, and community. The miracle of multiplication happens when what is in your hand meets what is in someone else's.

Think of the boy with the loaves and fishes. His little became much when it connected to divine purpose. The miracle did not happen in his hand; it happened in the hands of Jesus. When you release your seed into the right hands, you activate the supernatural law of partnership.

Partnership multiplies potential. What you lack, someone else carries. What they lack, you possess. When God joins divine purpose to human obedience, increase is inevitable. That is why isolation limits growth. God designed you to expand through connection.

But not every partnership produces. You must discern between covenant and convenience. Covenant partnerships are ordained by heaven; convenience partnerships are arranged by comfort. One multiplies, the other drains. Ask God to align you with those who share your vision, honour your values, and carry your faith.

When divine partnerships align, acceleration begins. Two can put ten thousand to flight because unity amplifies authority. Heaven blesses agreement. When hearts move in harmony, miracles move in motion. Increase thrives in the atmosphere of unity. That is why division is one of the enemy's favourite weapons. He knows that if he can isolate you, he can limit you. Guard your peace. Protect your unity.

Divine Wealth

Nurture relationships that bring you closer to purpose, not distraction.

As increase unfolds, it will test your motives. The greater your influence, the purer your intention must be. Increase reveals character. Wealth exposes what was already in your heart. If you were generous with little, you will be generous with much. If you were careless with little, abundance will magnify carelessness.

The law of increase carries responsibility. With every level of blessing comes a new level of stewardship. To manage more requires more wisdom, more humility, and more discernment. You cannot hold tomorrow's abundance with yesterday's mindset. Expansion demands evolution.

Growth will always require you to outgrow old versions of yourself. There will come moments when you must release familiar patterns, comfortable routines, and even certain people, to move into what God has next. Increase often feels like loss before it feels like gain. When Abraham obeyed God's call to leave his homeland, he stepped into uncertainty. Yet his obedience positioned him for overflow. God said, "I will make you into a great nation. I will bless you and make your name great, and through you all the families of the earth will be blessed." Abraham's increase began the moment he trusted what he could not see.

Faith is the currency of increase. You cannot purchase divine expansion with fear. Every step of faith is a seed that attracts favour. The moment you decide to trust God fully, you activate heaven's economy.

But faith is not merely belief; it is obedience in motion. You prove your faith by what you do, not just what you declare. The man who hears God's word and acts on it builds his house on rock. Storms may come, but foundations built on obedience never crumble.

Faith without works is lifeless potential. God increases those who walk, not those who wait in doubt. The Red Sea did not part until

Divine Wealth

Moses lifted his staff. The manna did not fall until Israel obeyed. The walls of Jericho did not collapse until the people marched. Increase follows movement.

Sometimes your step of faith will not make sense, but it will make history. Obedience often looks illogical to the natural mind. Yet every great move of God began with someone who dared to move first.

If you want to see supernatural increase, you must be willing to do something uncommon. Step out of comfort zones. Break away from limited thinking. Challenge traditions that no longer align with truth. God increases innovators, risk-takers, and vision carriers who dare to believe Him beyond the ordinary.

The law of increase also operates through generosity. The more you give, the more room you create to receive. Giving is not subtraction; it is multiplication in motion. Scripture says, "Give, and it shall be given unto you, good measure, pressed down, shaken together, and running over." God multiplies the open hand.

Every time you give, you declare that you trust the Giver more than the gift. You release your seed, not out of obligation, but out of revelation. You understand that the soil of faith always returns more than it receives.

Generosity keeps your heart soft and your hands open. It keeps you from worshipping what was meant to serve you. When you give, you stay free from the grip of greed and open to the flow of grace.

There is a rhythm in God's economy , sowing, growing, and reaping. When you live in that rhythm, increase becomes inevitable. Every act of giving becomes a doorway to new dimensions of blessing. You do not give to get; you give to grow. You give because you understand that in God's kingdom, nothing leaves your life that He cannot multiply.

When you give joyfully, heaven gives generously. When you give strategically, heaven gives supernaturally. Your seed may leave your

Divine Wealth

hand, but it never leaves your life. It travels into your future, waiting to meet you at your next harvest.

As increase begins to overflow, you must also learn the art of rest. Rest is not the absence of work; it is the presence of trust. The law of increase flows best in a peaceful heart. Anxiety blocks blessing, but rest invites revelation.

Rest is not inactivity; it is intentional stillness. It is the confidence that God is working behind the scenes. When you rest in His promises, you stop striving for what is already secured. You begin to experience a peace that is not dependent on possessions but anchored in purpose.

Increase without peace is emptiness. Abundance without contentment is chaos. The true blessing of increase is not just in what you gain, but in who you become through it.

The final dimension of the law of increase is overflow. Overflow is not about excess; it is about expression. God blesses you to be a blessing. He fills your cup so that others may drink from it. True overflow always flows outward.

Overflow turns your business into ministry, your home into refuge, your influence into impact. It transforms wealth into worship. You become a living testimony of divine generosity.

The law of increase always ends where it began , in the heart. A heart that believes, a heart that gives, a heart that trusts, a heart that worships. When your heart stays aligned with heaven, your life becomes the garden where God's abundance flourishes.

So, enlarge your vision. Expand your expectation. Dare to believe that God is not finished with your story. You are not at the edge of exhaustion; you are at the brink of expansion. The God who multiplied loaves, filled nets, and turned water into wine is still the same today.

He is ready to multiply what you believe for, but He waits for you to open the jar, to stretch the nets, to pour the oil, to step in faith.

Divine Wealth

When you do, you will discover that increase is not about arriving somewhere new, but about awakening something eternal. The seed of increase is already inside you, planted by the Creator Himself. Your belief waters it, your obedience grows it, and your surrender releases it.

This is the Kingdom law of increase , not a theory, but a truth, not a secret, but a song, not a transaction, but a transformation. It is God taking what you believe and turning it into what you become.

So walk boldly into your season of expansion. Stand firm in faith, give with joy, build with excellence, and rest in peace. For when your faith aligns with His purpose, there is no limit to what God can do through you.

You are the vessel of divine increase. The promise is not just for you; it is through you. And as you live in this truth, may your life overflow with grace, abundance, and glory that points every heart back to Him.

Divine Wealth

Chapter 5: The Currency of Faith: Living in Heaven's Economy on Earth

Divine Wealth

Faith is the currency of heaven. It is the medium through which the unseen becomes seen, the invisible becomes tangible, and the impossible becomes possible. Faith is not a feeling, nor a fleeting hope; it is the spiritual transaction through which the resources of heaven are transferred into the realities of earth.

In the world, money moves markets. In the Kingdom, faith moves mountains. The systems of this world operate on buying and selling, but the Kingdom of God operates on believing and receiving. To live by faith is to step into a higher economy, one that does not bend to inflation or fear, but thrives on trust and obedience.

Heaven's economy is not subject to earthly recessions. It is not shaken by headlines or hindered by circumstances. Its strength is found in one unchanging truth , that God remains faithful. When you anchor your life in faith, you plug into a source that cannot fail. Faith makes you recession-proof, fear-proof, and failure-proof, because it connects you to the One who owns it all.

Everything in creation operates by faith. Faith is the language of divine transaction, the bridge between heaven's intention and earthly manifestation. The moment you believe, something begins to shift. The moment you speak in alignment with what you believe, the unseen starts to respond.

Scripture says, "Without faith, it is impossible to please God." Faith is not merely an option; it is the oxygen of the Kingdom. Without it, nothing moves. Without it, nothing multiplies. Faith is what gives form to grace. Grace is the gift; faith is the hand that receives it.

The world says, "Seeing is believing." Heaven says, "Believing is seeing." Faith does not wait for evidence; it creates it. Faith speaks to what is not yet visible and calls it forth with conviction. Faith is not passive optimism; it is active expectation. It is not wishful thinking; it is spiritual knowing.

To live in heaven's economy, you must learn to trade in its currency. You cannot spend fear and expect abundance. You cannot transact

Divine Wealth

with doubt and expect divine increase. Faith is what opens the vaults of provision, the storehouses of heaven, and the wells of wisdom that never run dry.

The reason faith feels so radical is that it requires you to detach from the logic of lack. Faith asks you to see beyond what is, into what can be. It invites you to believe that the God who spoke galaxies into being is still speaking into your life today. Faith is not denial of reality; it is domination over limitation. It does not ignore facts; it overrides them with truth.

When you walk by faith, you begin to live as though heaven's supply is already present, even when your hands feel empty. You stop measuring your possibilities by your resources and start measuring them by God's character. You learn to say, "I may not see it yet, but I believe it already."

Faith is not born in comfort. It grows in tension. It is forged in moments of uncertainty when the only thing left to hold is God's promise. It is in those moments that faith becomes real , when everything else fades, and you realise that His word is enough.

Faith is the courage to walk on water while the storm still rages. It is the conviction that God's word carries more weight than the wind. It is the quiet confidence that though you cannot see the shore, the One who called you will not let you sink.

When Peter stepped out of the boat, he didn't walk on water; he walked on a word. One word from God carries more power than a thousand plans. That is why faith must always be rooted in revelation. You cannot believe beyond what you know of God. The strength of your faith will always mirror the depth of your intimacy with Him. Faith grows in fellowship. The more you hear His voice, the more you trust His heart. Faith comes by hearing, and hearing by the Word of God. This is not just about hearing with your ears, but about hearing with your spirit , that deep, sacred awareness that God is speaking directly to you.

Divine Wealth

When faith becomes your currency, fear loses its grip. You stop chasing certainty and start resting in divine assurance. You stop calculating outcomes and start trusting instructions. You move from striving to flowing, from anxiety to alignment.

Faith teaches you to live in two realms , the seen and the unseen. You begin to understand that reality is not limited to what is visible. The physical world is simply the shadow of the spiritual one. Faith is the lens that brings that higher reality into focus.

When you live by faith, you stop reacting to circumstances and start responding to calling. You stop letting scarcity dictate your steps and start letting the Spirit lead your strategy. You move from being controlled by what you see to being guided by what you believe.

Heaven's economy does not reward effort alone; it rewards expectation. Effort without faith exhausts you; faith without effort expands you. When faith fuels your work, grace multiplies your results. You begin to experience the supernatural efficiency of divine partnership , when your little becomes much in His hands.

The world calls it coincidence; heaven calls it orchestration. Faith aligns you with divine timing. You start to find yourself in the right places at the right moments, meeting the right people, receiving the right opportunities. These are not accidents; they are appointments prepared by God for those who trust Him enough to walk by faith.

Faith is a magnet for miracles. It draws heaven's possibilities into earthly reality. Every time you choose to believe, you release power. Every time you speak faith, you set the atmosphere for breakthrough. The Bible says, "According to your faith, let it be done unto you." Not according to your effort, not according to your status, but according to your faith.

Faith is what turns your wilderness into a well, your emptiness into overflow, your trial into testimony. Faith does not promise an easy path, but it guarantees a victorious destination.

Divine Wealth

The economy of heaven is generous, but it is not reckless. It entrusts abundance only to those who walk in obedience. Faith without obedience is fantasy. The moment you believe, God will give you an instruction , something to act on, something to move toward, something to release.

Every miracle in scripture required participation. The widow had to pour her oil. The blind man had to wash his eyes. The paralysed man had to pick up his mat. The lepers had to walk toward the priest. God never performs miracles without human movement. Faith is not magic; it is motion.

The law of heaven's economy is simple: what you move toward by faith, moves toward you by grace. You cannot stay still and expect increase. You must take a step. That step might be small, but it shifts the atmosphere.

When you move in faith, heaven responds. Angels are dispatched. Doors begin to open. Ideas start to flow. Divine connections are formed. What was once impossible becomes inevitable.

Faith does not wait for perfect conditions; it creates them. If you wait until you feel ready, you will never begin. Faith begins before you are ready, because readiness is revealed in movement, not in waiting.

There will always be voices of doubt , internal and external , telling you it cannot be done. But faith does not negotiate with fear; it silences it with truth. The more you feed your faith, the quieter your fear becomes.

Faith is contagious. When others see you walk in it, it ignites something within them. Your courage becomes their confirmation. Your testimony becomes their template. That is how the Kingdom grows , one act of faith inspiring another.

When faith becomes the currency of your life, lack loses its voice. You begin to operate from abundance, not anxiety. You start to see giving not as loss, but as leverage. You start to view challenges not as setbacks, but as setups.

Divine Wealth

Heaven's economy never runs out because it flows through a God who is limitless. The more you believe, the more capacity you create for His blessings to flow. The more you trust, the more territory you gain. Faith is the key that unlocks infinite resources.

Living in heaven's economy is not about escaping responsibility; it is about engaging faith responsibly. It is about understanding that God is not your banker; He is your partner. He is not merely funding your vision; He is forming your heart.

Faith calls you to see every season as sacred. The waiting season, the growing season, the stretching season, and the harvesting season all serve your destiny. Faith redeems time by giving every moment meaning.

When you look back, you begin to see how the pieces fit, how every delay built endurance, how every closed door redirected you toward better, how every hardship hid a higher purpose. Faith connects the dots of your destiny.

Heaven's economy is sustained by gratitude. Gratitude is the language of faith. The moment you thank God in advance, you prove your belief in His goodness. Gratitude multiplies grace because it shifts your focus from what is missing to what is present.

Faith and gratitude are divine twins. Where one grows, the other follows. Gratitude fuels expectation, and expectation fuels manifestation. When you thank God for what you have, you create room for more.

Faith teaches you that you already have everything you need for the next step. God will never ask you for what He has not already provided. The resources may not yet be visible, but they exist in seed form. Faith sees seeds where others see scarcity.

When you live by faith, you realise that miracles are not rare; they are the natural result of trust. The supernatural becomes the standard for those who believe. Every day becomes an opportunity to witness God's generosity in motion.

Divine Wealth

Faith transforms ordinary days into divine appointments. It turns routine tasks into sacred assignments. It turns the workplace into a mission field, the home into a sanctuary, the marketplace into a ministry.

Faith invites you to live differently , to see differently, speak differently, and expect differently. It changes how you view wealth, purpose, and even time itself. When you walk in faith, you begin to live not just chronologically, but spiritually , guided by seasons, not schedules.

The economy of faith is eternal. It cannot collapse because it is built on the integrity of God. The markets of men may rise and fall, but the promises of God remain constant.

Faith is the currency that never depreciates. It gains value every time you use it.

Faith not only opens the heavens, it changes the way you walk upon the earth. When faith becomes your foundation, you stop reacting to storms and start resting in promises. You no longer ask if God will come through; you begin to ask how He will choose to reveal His goodness this time. Faith shifts your questions from fear to expectation, from "Will it work?" to "What miracle will God do through this?"

Faith is not limited to moments of desperation; it is meant to be the rhythm of your daily life. It is the way you think, the way you speak, the way you move. Living in faith is not about waiting for breakthroughs; it is about walking as if they have already begun. It is the posture of the soul that refuses to doubt, even when evidence seems absent.

Faith is not the denial of difficulty; it is the declaration of victory in the midst of it. You do not ignore the mountain; you tell it to move. You do not close your eyes to the storm; you command peace to rise within it. When you live by faith, you begin to realise that your words

Divine Wealth

carry weight, because they echo the authority of the One who spoke creation into existence.

God has designed His Kingdom to function through faith, and faith alone. It is His chosen system of exchange, the divine method by which He partners with humanity. He does not respond to fear, status, or logic; He responds to faith. Faith speaks the language of heaven, and heaven always answers its own tongue.

Faith is spiritual currency, but it is also spiritual sight. It allows you to see beyond the moment, to look into eternity and draw its reality into the present. Every time you believe, you are bridging time itself, pulling tomorrow's miracle into today's obedience.

When Jesus said, "Your faith has made you whole," He was revealing that faith does not merely heal; it completes. It restores what was missing, repairs what was broken, and realigns what was misplaced. Faith makes you whole, not just in body, but in purpose, peace, and power.

The reason faith is powerful is because it agrees with God. Faith does not beg; it aligns. It does not attempt to convince God to act; it positions you to receive what He has already provided. God is not withholding blessings, He is waiting for alignment. Faith is alignment in motion.

To live by faith means to live above reaction. It means to operate from revelation, not emotion. The world lives by sight, but the believer lives by insight. Sight shows you what is; faith reveals what can be.

Faith transforms how you see everything. Problems become platforms, delays become preparation, and pain becomes power. What once intimidated you now instructs you. What once broke you now builds you. Because faith changes not just your circumstances, but your perception of them.

Faith teaches you that lack is not loss; it is invitation. Every gap in your life is an opportunity for God to show Himself faithful. Where

Divine Wealth

you see emptiness, heaven sees potential. Where you see delay, heaven sees development. Every season of waiting is a classroom for growth.

God uses the waiting room to strengthen the muscles of your faith. He allows you to walk through uncertainty so that your trust may deepen. Faith that has never been tested will always be shallow. But faith that has weathered storms becomes unshakable. The winds that once terrified you become the very forces that carry you higher.

Faith matures through pressure. It is easy to believe when the sun shines, but it is in the darkness that faith discovers its voice. It is in the silence that faith learns to sing. When you can still praise in uncertainty, still trust when answers are delayed, still give when resources feel low, then you have stepped into mature faith.

Mature faith does not panic; it persists. It does not rush; it rests. It does not collapse under contradiction; it holds on to conviction. Mature faith says, "Even if He does not do it now, He is still good." God is not moved by panic; He is moved by persistence. The woman with the issue of blood did not receive healing because she had status, wealth, or influence. She received it because her faith refused to let go. Her determination turned desperation into destiny. She reached beyond logic and touched grace.

Every act of faith carries a reach. Faith does not wait politely; it presses persistently. It pushes through crowds of doubt, distractions, and disappointments, reaching for the hem of His garment. When you reach in faith, heaven always responds.

Faith breaks protocol. It does not wait for permission to believe. It crosses boundaries, challenges expectations, and redefines what is possible. God honours bold faith, the kind that dares to believe before it sees.

Faith does not ask "if," it declares "when." It lives from the certainty that God cannot lie. His promises are not fragile; they are eternal.

Divine Wealth

Every word He has spoken carries power, and that power does not diminish with time.

The economy of heaven runs on the integrity of God. His Word is the currency, His character the guarantee. Faith is the receipt of things hoped for, the evidence of things not yet seen. When you have faith, you already possess the proof of what others are still waiting for.

Faith is a lifestyle of trust. It teaches you to see beyond the surface, to live by divine supply instead of visible shortage. It causes you to look at your empty nets and still cast them into the deep.

Peter had fished all night and caught nothing, yet at the word of Jesus, he tried again. Faith tries again. Faith sows again. Faith dreams again. The first attempt may have failed, but faith never stops expecting favour.

The miraculous catch did not come because the lake suddenly filled with fish; it came because obedience created opportunity. Faith does not change God's willingness; it changes your position. When you move in faith, you move into alignment with divine abundance.

Faith never leaves you where it found you. It elevates, enlarges, and empowers. It shifts your identity from victim to victor, from seeker to steward, from borrower to builder. Faith reveals that you were never created to survive; you were designed to thrive.

Faith is the soil in which destiny grows. It is the foundation upon which every promise stands. Without faith, blessings stay dormant, but with faith, they burst into bloom.

The life of faith requires continual renewal. You cannot live today on yesterday's revelation. Manna that fed you yesterday will not sustain you tomorrow. Faith must be fresh, because faith flows from relationship. The closer you walk with God, the clearer your hearing becomes.

Faith flourishes in intimacy. The more you know Him, the easier it becomes to trust Him. When you understand His nature, you no

Divine Wealth

longer question His timing. You begin to see that delays are not denials; they are designs.

Faith teaches you that God's silence is not His absence. Silence is often the sound of construction. When God appears quiet, He is often building what you have prayed for behind the scenes.

The greatest miracles often unfold slowly. Seeds do not shout as they grow; they stretch silently beneath the soil. Faith is patient enough to let God finish what He started.

Faith also carries fragrance. It attracts heaven's attention and leaves a trail of testimony behind it. Wherever faith has walked, miracles follow.

Heaven honours movement, not mere intention. God rewards those who diligently seek Him, not casually consider Him. Faith is diligence dressed in devotion. It is the consistency to pray when you feel nothing, to give when you have little, to believe when you see nothing.

Faith lives in action, but it rests in assurance. It does not hustle for validation; it lives validated by grace.

Faith reminds you that you do not need all the answers to take the next step. You just need the confidence that the One who called you holds the map. Each act of obedience reveals the next direction. God does not show the whole picture; He gives you one frame at a time, because faith grows through trust, not control.

The more you practice faith, the less you panic in uncertainty. You begin to see challenges as invitations to trust deeper. The moments that once made you anxious now make you alert, because you know something divine is about to unfold.

Faith sharpens your spiritual sensitivity. You start to notice God's fingerprints in the smallest details. You realise that there are no coincidences, only confirmations.

Faith trains your heart to hear the rhythm of heaven. You stop rushing ahead and start walking in sync with divine timing. When you

Divine Wealth

move too fast, you outrun grace. When you move too slow, you delay growth. But when you move in rhythm with faith, everything aligns perfectly.

Faith is timing in trust. It is peace in waiting, motion in believing, stillness in surrender.

Heaven's economy runs on rhythm, sowing and reaping, waiting and witnessing, trusting and thanking. When you live in rhythm with heaven, your life begins to overflow naturally.

Faith is also contagious in community. The presence of faithful people multiplies courage. When believers gather in one spirit, their faith becomes a collective force that breaks barriers. Unity in faith invites divine manifestation.

When the early church prayed in one accord, the place shook. When Paul and Silas sang in the prison, chains fell off. When people gather in agreement, heaven releases acceleration.

Faith is never solitary; it is strengthened in fellowship. It grows when shared, expands when expressed, and multiplies when modelled. That is why testimonies matter , they are seeds of faith sown into other hearts.

When you share what God has done, you create expectation in others. What He did for one, He can do for all. Faith thrives on remembrance. Every testimony is evidence that God remains faithful.

Faith is also generous. It does not hoard miracles; it multiplies them. When you live by faith, you become a channel of blessing. The same faith that brings provision into your life empowers you to release it into others.

Faith breaks the cycle of scarcity because it teaches you that giving is not loss; it is planting. Every seed you release in faith grows into a harvest that benefits many.

As faith matures, it becomes less about what you get and more about who you become. You begin to realise that faith is not just for

Divine Wealth

prosperity; it is for purpose. It aligns your heart with heaven so that everything you do becomes worship.

Faith turns ordinary obedience into extraordinary outcomes. It transforms small acts into significant impact. When you give, serve, or speak in faith, you shift atmospheres. The unseen begins to rearrange itself to accommodate your obedience.

Faith is not loud, but it is powerful. It may whisper, yet it moves mountains. It may begin as a mustard seed, yet it grows into a forest of possibility.

Every time you choose faith, the heavens respond. You align yourself with eternal flow. You participate in the very rhythm that holds galaxies together. You become a living echo of divine creation, speaking life where there was loss, hope where there was despair, abundance where there was lack.

Faith is not just belief; it is belonging. It connects you to the heartbeat of heaven, making you a co-labourer with God. When you believe, you join Him in the work of creation.

Faith transforms you into a vessel of divine economy. It teaches you to live with open hands, open eyes, and an open heart. You stop chasing the provision and start walking with the Provider.

This is the secret of heaven's economy: God never runs out of what you need. His supply is infinite, His generosity endless, His timing perfect. Faith keeps you connected to that flow, ensuring that no season of your life is ever without purpose or provision.

So, live by faith. Speak with faith. Build with faith. Give with faith. Love with faith. Let every part of your life become a reflection of your trust in God's goodness.

Faith is not what you have; it is who you are when you remember who He is.

When faith becomes your way of life, lack loses its language, fear loses its footing, and heaven finds expression through you.

Divine Wealth

You are heaven's investment on earth, and faith is your divine currency. Spend it boldly, sow it freely, and watch as God turns your belief into beauty, your hope into harvest, and your trust into transformation.

Divine Wealth

Chapter 6: The Law of Divine Timing: Trusting God's Pace for Your Prosperity

Divine Wealth

Timing is the silent language of heaven. It speaks in pauses and patterns, in seasons and stillness, in moments that seem delayed but are deeply deliberate. When you learn to move with divine timing, you stop striving for control and start resting in rhythm. You begin to understand that God's pace is not a punishment; it is protection. What feels like delay is often divine design.

Every promise has a season, and every seed has a cycle. Faith may plant the seed, but timing brings the harvest. To rush what God is still shaping is to risk receiving what is not yet ready. Divine timing ensures that blessings arrive not when you want them, but when you can sustain them.

Impatience is the enemy of divine order. The world moves in haste, but heaven moves in harmony. You can force a door open with effort, but only timing will keep it open with grace. God's timing is not about postponement; it is about preparation. It refines your motives, tests your endurance, and strengthens your character until you can carry what you prayed for.

When you truly trust God's timing, you stop asking "when" and start asking "what." What are You teaching me, Lord? What are You preparing in me? What must grow before the blessing grows? Divine timing is never random; it is deeply relational. It aligns your growth with your grace.

There are moments when it seems as though God has forgotten you, when the silence stretches too long, and the wait becomes heavy. Yet it is in those moments that heaven does its deepest work. Silence is not absence; it is formation. When God is quiet, He is often constructing the stage for your next season.

We live in an age obsessed with immediacy. Everything around us promises instant results , instant success, instant gratification, instant validation. But the Kingdom does not operate on human clocks. It runs on eternal calendars, where maturity takes precedence over

Divine Wealth

speed. What comes quickly often fades quickly. What is forged through faith lasts forever.

Abraham waited decades for Isaac. Joseph endured years in captivity before stepping into leadership. David was anointed as king long before he ever wore a crown. Each of them carried a promise that took time to mature. Delay did not mean denial; it meant development. God was not punishing them by making them wait; He was preparing them to reign.

Every divine delay is purposeful. God will never give you something meant to bless you in a season that could break you. The waiting is not wasted. It shapes you, humbles you, teaches you dependence. Waiting purifies your motives and transforms desire into devotion. When you trust divine timing, you learn to see waiting not as stagnation but as cultivation. The soil of patience is where faith grows deep roots. Every season of waiting has a lesson, and those who learn the lesson inherit the promise.

You cannot rush revelation. You cannot demand destiny. God's process cannot be hurried, because it is not mechanical; it is relational. You are not just a participant in His plan; you are a partner in His process.

There is a sacred rhythm to divine timing. You plant in faith, water in perseverance, and harvest in joy. But between planting and harvesting lies the mystery of time. That space between the promise and its fulfillment is where your heart learns to trust, your patience learns to endure, and your obedience learns to stay steady.

The beauty of divine timing is that it redeems every season. Nothing is wasted in God's calendar. The moments that felt like detours were actually directions. The delays that seemed discouraging were divine detours guiding you toward destiny.

There is a peace that comes from knowing that you cannot miss what God has ordained for you. You may feel behind, but in heaven's eyes, you are right on time. The world compares timelines, but heaven

Divine Wealth

designs journeys. Your path is not meant to mirror another's; it is meant to magnify God's unique work in you.

Divine timing requires surrender. It asks you to release your deadlines and embrace God's direction. It demands faith that trusts even when logic disagrees. It teaches you to breathe in peace when progress feels slow, and to rest in assurance when results are unseen.

Waiting is not inactivity; it is inner work. When you wait on God, you are not standing still; you are growing still. You are building the strength that stillness requires, the kind that anchors you when blessings begin to flow.

Impatience often masks insecurity. We hurry because we fear missing out, but nothing aligned with God's plan can bypass you. When the time is right, the opportunity will find you. The blessing will knock on your door because divine timing never loses its way.

There are seasons when God accelerates, and seasons when He slows you down. Acceleration without preparation can be dangerous. Slowing down without revelation can feel frustrating. But when you align with God's pace, both acceleration and stillness become sacred. Divine timing is like the tide. When the tide recedes, it is not retreating; it is gathering strength. When it returns, it carries abundance. Some seasons pull you back so that others can propel you forward. Do not mistake divine withdrawal for divine abandonment. What God withholds for a season, He multiplies in the next.

When you live according to heaven's timing, you begin to understand that purpose has its own clock. It cannot be manipulated or manufactured. You cannot force fruit to ripen, but when it does, it is sweet, strong, and lasting.

Faith and timing are inseparable. Faith teaches you to believe; timing teaches you to wait. Together, they build the balance that every believer needs. To have faith without patience is to have a seed without soil. To have patience without faith is to have soil without seed. But when both coexist, miracles manifest.

Divine Wealth

Divine timing requires you to release comparison. The enemy of peace is the illusion of someone else's pace. You do not know what God is doing in another's process. Their breakthrough is not your benchmark. God's timeline for you is tailored to your assignment. Comparing your chapter one to another's chapter twenty is a theft of joy.

There is a grace that flows when you stop competing and start cultivating. You learn to celebrate others without resenting your own waiting. The success of another believer is not a threat to your calling; it is a testimony of what is possible when faith and timing unite. When you live in alignment with divine timing, anxiety gives way to assurance. You no longer pray from panic; you pray from peace. You no longer chase doors; you prepare for them. You begin to understand that closed doors are not rejection; they are redirection. God will close doors that lead to distraction. He will block opportunities that would break your focus. Every "no" you hear is guarding a greater "yes." Trusting His timing means believing that His denial is also His protection.

Sometimes divine timing feels inconvenient. It interrupts your plans, shifts your expectations, and challenges your patience. Yet it is always perfect. You may not understand it now, but when you look back, every delay will make sense. You will see how each detour was directing you to destiny.

Divine timing is not about arrival; it is about alignment. God is not trying to get you there faster; He is preparing you to stay there longer. Quick success can become quick failure without the character to sustain it. Timing protects you from becoming overwhelmed by what you are not yet equipped to carry.

Every promise requires preparation. You cannot inherit what you have not yet matured into. God's timing ensures that your blessing does not destroy you. The waiting room of faith is the gymnasium of the spirit, where endurance, humility, and gratitude are strengthened.

Divine Wealth

There is a peace that only comes when you surrender the calendar. When you let go of your need to know when and start trusting the One who already knows how, life begins to flow again. The anxiety of control is replaced by the assurance of faith.

Divine timing often feels slower than you wish but faster than you think. It moves at the pace of purpose, not preference. When God delays, it is never to diminish you, but to deepen you.

The heart that trusts divine timing is unshakeable. It does not crumble under uncertainty, because it knows that uncertainty is the soil where faith blooms. It does not despair when plans shift, because it understands that detours often lead to destinations that direct paths could never reach.

Every believer must learn the sacred art of waiting well. Waiting well means worshipping while you wait, serving while you stay still, believing while you build. It means not losing enthusiasm when progress feels slow, because you know that growth is happening underground.

Waiting is not wasted time; it is sacred time. It is the womb where destiny develops. It is where vision matures and faith strengthens. When the time comes, everything will happen suddenly, but that suddenness will be the fruit of seasons of faithfulness. Divine acceleration always follows divine preparation.

The moment the appointed time arrives, no power in heaven or earth can stop it. What once felt impossible becomes effortless. What once required striving now flows with grace.

That is the mystery of divine timing. It teaches you that God's "not yet" is still a promise, not a refusal. It reminds you that if it is delayed, it is because it is being designed. If it has not arrived, it is because it is still being arranged.

Trust that while you wait, heaven works. God is orchestrating what you cannot yet see. He is aligning hearts, resources, and

Divine Wealth

opportunities. He is preparing people you have not met and paths you have not walked.

In divine timing, everything connects. What once seemed random becomes revelation. What once felt wasted becomes woven into your purpose.

Divine timing is not slow; it is strategic. It ensures that when the blessing comes, it fits perfectly.

You are not behind. You are being built. You are not delayed. You are being developed. Every moment is moving you toward manifestation.

To live in divine timing is to live in rhythm with eternity. When you begin to understand that every season carries a sacred purpose, your impatience transforms into peace. You stop wrestling against the current of God's process and begin to flow with it. You start to see that what feels like stillness is often strategy, and what feels like delay is often design.

God is not bound by clocks or calendars. He does not rush because you are restless, nor does He stall because you are steady. He moves according to purpose, not pressure. His plans are not fragile; they are eternal. When you trust His pace, you begin to see that His timing is not just perfect , it is personal. It is shaped specifically for you, tailored for your journey, measured by your destiny.

There is a reason some doors do not open when you knock, and some opportunities seem to slip away. God's "not yet" is not a rejection; it is a redirection. Sometimes He closes a door because you are not meant to enter it , you are meant to build your own. Divine timing protects you from settling for what looks good when something greater is still being prepared.

The law of divine timing teaches that God prepares blessings as carefully as He prepares believers. It is not enough for the door to be ready; you must be ready too. A blessing received before maturity can

Divine Wealth

become a burden. That is why God takes His time, because He is shaping your character to match your calling.

Your preparation season is sacred. The hidden years are not punishment; they are formation. These are the seasons when God refines your motives, strengthens your foundation, and sharpens your focus. When nothing seems to move, heaven is often moving the most.

Look at David, tending sheep while carrying a king's anointing. His years in the fields were not wasted; they were training for the throne. Look at Joseph, unjustly imprisoned yet being prepared to rule a nation. The waiting room is where faith graduates into wisdom. What God develops in private, He later displays in power.

If you are in a season of stillness, do not despise it. Stillness is not stagnation. It is the space where purpose takes shape. While you wait, worship. While you serve, listen. While you build quietly, heaven is positioning you publicly. Divine timing does not just reward faith; it rewards faithfulness.

Many lose heart because they mistake movement for progress. But in God's economy, stillness can be the greatest sign of advancement. Waiting trains you to depend not on momentum, but on maturity. It teaches you that growth is not always visible, but it is always happening.

When the time comes, everything that seemed delayed will suddenly align. What felt impossible will unfold with ease. Divine timing brings acceleration without striving. It compresses years into moments. It redeems what was lost and restores what was broken.

Sometimes God waits until everything else has failed so that when the breakthrough comes, there is no question about who deserves the glory. Delay reveals dependence. It proves that what you are building is not powered by effort alone, but sustained by grace.

In divine timing, your seasons are not wasted; they are woven. God interlaces every thread of your life into a tapestry of purpose. What

Divine Wealth

you thought was a setback was a stitch in your story. The pattern may not make sense now, but one day you will see how every colour, every tear, every delay formed something beautiful.

You will look back and realise that the timing was perfect all along. The detours taught humility, the pauses taught patience, and the disappointments built depth. Divine timing rarely feels comfortable, but it always produces completeness.

To trust divine timing is to release control. It is to wake up each day and say, "Lord, I will move when You move. I will rest when You rest. I will trust when I do not understand." Trust is not just belief; it is surrender. It is the willingness to say yes even when the outcome is unseen.

When you trust God's pace, you stop trying to manufacture miracles. You no longer manipulate circumstances to make things happen. Instead, you learn to align, to prepare, to stay ready. Divine timing meets those who remain faithful in the unseen.

God's timing is often revealed through peace. If you are forcing it, it is not Him. If you are striving, it is not now. The right door will not require you to compromise your character to enter it. Divine timing does not create confusion; it confirms calling. It brings clarity, harmony, and ease.

There will come a moment when God whispers, "Now." That moment will be unmistakable. The doors will open without struggle, the path will clear, and grace will flow like water. All that waiting, all that pressing, all that faith will converge in a single, divine moment of release.

When that time comes, you will not need to chase it, it will chase you. You will not need to knock on doors; they will open at your approach. You will not need to explain yourself; your fruit will speak for you. That is the beauty of divine timing. It carries the weight of heaven's endorsement.

Divine Wealth

Those who learn to wait in faith also learn to move in obedience. The same faith that teaches you to pause must also teach you to proceed. When God says go, hesitation becomes disobedience. Trusting His timing means staying still when He says wait, and moving swiftly when He says move.

Divine timing has two tests: patience and readiness. Patience sustains you while you wait; readiness positions you for when the moment arrives. Many lose opportunities not because they were unworthy, but because they were unprepared. Faith without readiness misses divine windows.

The wise believer learns to prepare while waiting. Noah built the ark before the rain. Joseph planned for famine before it arrived. Faith always builds in advance. When God gives you a promise, begin preparing for it as though it were already unfolding. That preparation becomes your prophetic act of trust.

Sometimes divine timing arrives suddenly, like lightning that splits the sky. Other times it unfolds gently, like dawn breaking after a long night. Whether slow or swift, it always comes right on time. God never misses His own appointments.

Living in rhythm with divine timing transforms how you approach life. You stop rushing through seasons. You start discerning them. You learn to ask, "Lord, is this a planting season, a pruning season, or a harvesting season?" Each one requires a different posture of the heart.

The planting season is about sowing in faith. You give, serve, and believe, even when there is no visible return. The pruning season is about letting go of what no longer bears fruit , old habits, old fears, old ways of thinking. The harvest season is about stewardship, learning to handle abundance with humility and wisdom.

Every believer will cycle through these seasons many times. The secret is to discern which one you are in and to honour it. A farmer does not demand fruit in winter. He knows that winter prepares the

Divine Wealth

soil for spring. In the same way, your seasons of seeming dormancy are preparing the roots for future growth.

Divine timing teaches rhythm, and rhythm brings rest. You begin to understand that the pressure to perform is replaced by the peace of partnership. You are not trying to make life happen; you are allowing life to happen through you. You move with grace, not with grind.

The moment you align with God's timing, everything begins to flow. Opportunities connect, relationships align, ideas ignite. Things that once required striving begin to unfold naturally. You stop chasing, and you start attracting.

This is not coincidence; it is convergence. When your spirit is in rhythm with God, heaven collaborates with your effort. Your steps become ordered, your vision becomes clear, and your progress becomes purposeful.

Divine timing also brings divine favour. Favour is not luck; it is alignment. It is the manifestation of being in the right place, at the right time, with the right heart. When timing and obedience meet, doors open that no man can shut.

Those who live by divine timing are never late to destiny. They do not fear being overlooked, because they know that grace always finds those who are faithful.

When you surrender to timing, you begin to experience the serenity of trust. You stop panicking about tomorrow and start praising for today. You realise that each day is both preparation and promise. You are not waiting for a better season; you are learning to walk faithfully in this one.

There will be moments when everything feels delayed, and others when everything happens at once. Both are sacred. Both are divine. The stillness teaches surrender; the acceleration teaches stewardship. In both, God is present, guiding, shaping, and stretching your faith. When your life aligns with divine timing, even your detours lead to destiny. What once seemed like a mistake becomes a miracle. What

Divine Wealth

once hurt becomes holy. You realise that nothing was wasted. Every pain had purpose, every pause had power.

Divine timing is not a lesson you master once; it is a rhythm you learn to live in daily. It requires listening, patience, and surrender. It asks you to live from peace, not pressure.

As you grow in this rhythm, you begin to live differently. You stop fighting the seasons and start flowing with them. You wake each day with calm assurance that God's plan is unfolding exactly as it should. When divine timing takes hold of your life, you become unshakeable. Storms may come, but they no longer steal your peace. Delays may happen, but they no longer breed despair. You walk with steady faith, knowing that the Author of time is writing your story with precision and love.

There will come a day when all the waiting, all the tears, all the wondering will make sense. You will look back and see that the thread of divine timing ran through it all. You will thank God for not letting things happen earlier, because now you will understand why later was better.

The law of divine timing reminds you that heaven is never late, and God never forgets. His timing is not random; it is redemptive. It restores, refines, and reveals. It ensures that every promise arrives dressed in perfection.

So, be still in the waiting, be bold in the believing, and be ready when the call comes. Your moment is on its way, not because you chased it, but because you trusted the One who sends it.

When your life aligns with God's timing, you live with effortless grace. You no longer force, you flow. You no longer strive, you surrender. You no longer worry, you worship.

And that is when the world begins to see the reflection of divine peace through you. You become the living proof that timing is not just about moments , it is about mastery. It is the art of trusting the

Divine Wealth

pace of heaven, the rhythm of grace, and the perfection of divine love.

Divine Wealth

Chapter 7: The Anointing of Increase: Walking in Divine Provision and Overflow

Divine Wealth

There comes a moment in every believer's life when God begins to whisper about more. Not just more things, but more capacity, more purpose, more impact. It is not a call to greed; it is a call to greatness. It is the invitation to step into the anointing of increase, the divine empowerment that multiplies what you carry until it touches the lives of others.

Increase is not simply about accumulation. It is about expansion. It is the stretching of your spirit, the enlarging of your vision, the awakening of your potential. It is God's way of saying that you were never meant to stay where you are. You were meant to grow, to build, to flourish, to manifest His glory in ever greater ways.

When the anointing of increase rests on your life, everything you touch begins to bear fruit. Opportunities open, ideas flow, doors unlock, and grace multiplies. This is not coincidence; it is covenant. God promised Abraham that He would bless him and make him a blessing. That same covenant flows through every believer who walks in faith.

Increase is not earned; it is entrusted. God gives abundance to those who understand that it is not about self-elevation but about Kingdom elevation. The anointing of increase is not a reward for ambition; it is a response to alignment. When your motives are pure, and your purpose is anchored in service, heaven releases resources to match your mission.

The world measures success by what you gather; heaven measures it by what you give. Divine increase is not about having more to possess; it is about having more to pour. When your heart becomes a channel, not a container, God never stops the flow.

There is a reason why Scripture calls God Jehovah Jireh, the Lord who provides. His nature is abundance, and His desire is multiplication. From the very beginning, His first words to humanity were a command of fruitfulness. "Be fruitful and multiply." That was

Divine Wealth

not merely biological instruction; it was spiritual mandate. You were designed for increase.

Yet increase begins within. Before God multiplies what is in your hands, He multiplies what is in your heart. He expands your faith, your vision, your endurance, and your obedience. He prepares you to handle what He intends to release. Many ask for abundance, but few prepare for it. Without inner growth, external increase becomes unsustainable.

The anointing of increase is activated when stewardship meets surrender. God does not bless wastefulness, but He multiplies wisdom. The same oil that flowed through the widow's jars in Scripture flowed only in the measure that she was willing to pour. The miracle was not in the oil; it was in her obedience.

Increase is not an event; it is an environment. It happens wherever faith, diligence, and gratitude coexist. When you create a space of faith through expectation, a space of diligence through action, and a space of gratitude through praise, heaven fills it with provision.

God's provision is not limited to material resources. It includes ideas, insights, connections, and creativity. The anointing of increase touches every area of life. It expands your influence, deepens your relationships, strengthens your leadership, and multiplies your joy. It is a total transformation, not a partial blessing.

To walk in divine increase, you must first dismantle the mindset of limitation. Scarcity is not a lack of resources; it is a lack of revelation. When you see yourself as limited, you restrict what God can do through you. When you recognise that you are a vessel of divine flow, you realise that the only limit is your level of belief.

The mind of Christ does not operate in lack. It operates in creativity, innovation, and abundance. When Jesus fed the multitudes with five loaves and two fish, He did not see shortage; He saw seed. He looked at what was in His hands, blessed it, and broke it. The blessing released multiplication, and the breaking released manifestation.

Divine Wealth

There is a profound truth in that moment. Increase often comes through breaking. The breaking of pride, the breaking of fear, the breaking of self-dependence. God breaks what you give Him, not to destroy it, but to distribute it. When you surrender what you have, He multiplies it beyond measure.

The anointing of increase flows where there is surrender. It is not activated by striving but by yielding. When you release control, you release capacity. The open hand receives more than the clenched fist. When you live with open hands, heaven trusts you with treasures.

Increase also requires integrity. God will not pour abundance into a vessel that leaks. Character is the container that holds blessing. Without it, what comes quickly will vanish just as quickly. Integrity keeps what favour brings.

The anointing of increase thrives in purity. When your intentions are pure, increase becomes effortless. When your motives are tainted by pride or greed, increase becomes heavy. God blesses those whose hearts remain humble in prosperity and grateful in plenty.

There is a posture that attracts increase, a heart that says, "Lord, whatever You give me, I will use for Your glory." When that becomes your declaration, heaven opens its storehouse. God looks for those who can carry increase without losing intimacy.

Every level of increase requires a new level of discipline. Abundance magnifies stewardship. If you cannot manage a little, you cannot maintain a lot. The same principle that governs faith also governs finances: those who are faithful in little will be rulers over much.

To walk in increase is to walk in responsibility. Blessing is not freedom from accountability; it is empowerment for greater service. God does not give you wealth to elevate status; He gives it to expand stewardship.

When you understand this, you stop asking for riches and start asking for revelation. You stop praying for possessions and start praying for

Divine Wealth

purpose. The truly wealthy are not those who have much, but those who know why they have it.

The anointing of increase is about divine partnership. God blesses those who build with Him. He provides resources to those who align their lives with Kingdom purpose. He releases wealth into hands that are committed to His work.

The greatest evidence of increase is generosity. True prosperity does not end with you; it flows through you. When you become a channel for God's abundance, you will never run dry. Giving is not subtraction; it is multiplication in motion.

Heaven's economy operates on circulation. The more you release, the more God replenishes. The more you sow, the more you grow. It is not magic; it is divine mathematics. The open heart and open hand create perpetual flow.

Increase has an atmosphere. It dwells where faith is alive, gratitude is constant, and giving is joyful. It cannot coexist with fear, resentment, or doubt. When you fill your environment with praise and purpose, you make room for provision.

The anointing of increase transforms your relationship with money. It teaches you that money is not the master; it is the messenger. It carries your values into the world. It becomes the tool by which purpose is manifested. Money in the hands of a believer is a servant of destiny.

When you understand that money is spiritual, you begin to handle it with holiness. You stop seeing it as something secular and start viewing it as sacred. Every dollar becomes a declaration of faith, a seed of impact, a testimony of stewardship.

Increase is also about alignment. You cannot walk in abundance while living in disobedience. Prosperity without purpose leads to emptiness. The anointing of increase flows only through channels that honour God.

Divine Wealth

When your life becomes an offering, everything you touch becomes blessed. Your work becomes worship. Your leadership becomes legacy. Your wealth becomes witness. That is the true power of divine increase , not accumulation, but transformation.

God's increase is not limited by circumstance. He blessed Isaac a hundredfold in the midst of famine. He provided manna in the desert, water from the rock, and oil from empty jars. Heaven's supply is not controlled by earth's conditions. When you walk under the anointing of increase, you live above the limitations of the world's systems.

There will always be those who do not understand divine increase. Some will call it arrogance; others will call it luck. But those who walk in revelation know that it is neither pride nor chance , it is grace. Grace that flows to those who believe, obey, and give.

To walk in divine increase is to live as a steward of supernatural abundance. It is to carry the confidence that God is not just enough; He is more than enough. It is to believe that your cup does not simply fill; it overflows, spilling into every life it touches.

Increase is the evidence of intimacy. When you walk closely with God, you cannot help but multiply. His presence produces prosperity, not because you chase wealth, but because you carry wisdom. Where He is, there is provision.

The anointing of increase is not about external display; it is about internal alignment. It is a heart posture, a spiritual frequency that attracts heaven's resources. When your heart beats in rhythm with God's generosity, abundance becomes your natural state.

Your increase is not for your comfort; it is for your calling. It is to feed the hungry, to uplift the broken, to build what will outlast you. Increase gives you influence, and influence gives you impact. The greater your capacity, the greater your calling to serve.

The true test of divine increase is how you use it. When you bless others with what you have, God entrusts you with more. When you

Divine Wealth

hoard what you have, you stop the flow. The law of increase always honours the giver.

The anointing of increase is not a one-time experience; it is a lifelong journey. It grows as you grow, expands as you expand, and deepens as your understanding matures. It is not just about receiving from God; it is about becoming a reflection of His nature.

God is abundance. He lacks nothing, and He withholds nothing good from those who walk uprightly. When His Spirit dwells in you, increase becomes inevitable. Not because of luck, but because of law , the law of faith, the law of giving, the law of gratitude.

When you walk under this anointing, you begin to see life differently. You see every challenge as a chance to grow, every opportunity as a divine assignment, every resource as a seed for the next miracle.

Increase is the language of a generous God. It is His way of saying, "I trust you with more because you were faithful with little."

The anointing of increase rests upon those who carry both humility and hunger , humility to remember where the blessing comes from, and hunger to use it for the good of others.

Your purpose is too great for scarcity. Your calling is too large for fear. You were never created to live in lack; you were created to live in overflow. The anointing of increase is the invitation to return to that original design , a life of abundance, service, and divine supply.

Overflow is not a state of possession; it is a state of presence. It is what happens when God's abundance within you exceeds the boundaries of your needs. It is the point where faith becomes fruit, where prayer becomes provision, and where generosity becomes the rhythm of your life. Overflow is not about excess; it is about expansion. It is the sign that what God placed in you has grown too large to remain contained.

When you live in overflow, you live in partnership with heaven. You no longer chase after blessings because blessings begin to follow you. The Scripture says, "Surely goodness and mercy shall follow me all

Divine Wealth

the days of my life." Overflow means that what used to be pursued now pursues you. It is divine momentum, the flow of favour that cannot be earned but can be positioned for.

Overflow begins with obedience. The river of God's increase always flows through the channel of obedience. When you move at His word, heaven moves on your behalf. Every miracle in Scripture began with obedience. "Fill the jars with water." "Cast your net on the right side." "Stretch out your hand." The instruction always preceded the increase.

When you live in obedience, you align yourself with divine flow. You become like a tree planted by streams of living water, bearing fruit in every season. Your leaves do not wither because your roots reach the Source. The key to sustained abundance is not striving; it is staying connected.

Many people pray for overflow but resist the pruning that produces it. Pruning is not punishment; it is preparation. God removes what no longer serves your purpose so that what remains can bear more fruit. Every branch that bears fruit, He prunes so it will bear even more. Increase without pruning becomes clutter, but pruning without increase becomes pain. When both work together, growth becomes inevitable.

The anointing of increase is not a one-time outpouring; it is a continual process. It grows as your faith grows. It deepens as your gratitude deepens. It matures as your stewardship matures. The more you honour what you have, the more God entrusts to your hands. Heaven's flow responds to honour.

Overflow also requires order. God will not fill what is disorganised. Before the miracle of the loaves and fish, Jesus told the people to sit down in groups. Before the oil flowed for the widow, she was told to gather vessels and shut the door. Order precedes outpouring. The vessel that is prepared is the one that gets filled.

Divine Wealth

You cannot expect overflow while neglecting discipline. Divine abundance thrives where there is structure. Budgeting, planning, sowing, and saving are spiritual acts when done with the right heart. Stewardship invites supply. When you show God you can manage increase, He multiplies it.

Overflow is not meant to end with you. It is meant to flow through you. It is the outward expression of inward faith. When you give, you make room for more. When you release what you have, heaven replenishes it. The world calls it generosity, but heaven calls it multiplication.

There is a rhythm to overflow, a divine circulation that mirrors the heartbeat of God. Inhale grace, exhale generosity. Receive favour, release faith. Take in blessing, give out blessing. The flow never stops because the vessel never closes.

When you begin to live this way, money becomes light instead of weight. It loses its power to control and gains its purpose to contribute. You begin to see money not as a goal, but as a tool, not as a symbol of success, but as a seed of service.

The anointing of increase changes your relationship with giving. Giving stops being an obligation and becomes a joy. You give not because you must, but because you trust. You know that every seed sown in love will return in abundance. You give because you have discovered the secret of divine economics: generosity multiplies.

The more you give, the more you grow. The more you release, the more you receive. Not because of transaction, but because of transformation. Giving enlarges the heart. It expands your capacity for love and empathy. It teaches you that abundance is not measured by what you keep, but by what you release.

To live in overflow is to live in gratitude. Gratitude is the soil where increase takes root. It turns little into enough and enough into more. Gratitude is not a reaction to blessing; it is the environment that

Divine Wealth

attracts it. When your heart is full of thankfulness, your hands will never be empty.

There is power in praising God for what has not yet come. Faith-filled gratitude creates magnetic energy in the spirit. It draws provision toward you because it shows heaven that you already believe. Gratitude is faith in its purest form. It says, "Lord, I thank You, not just for what I see, but for what I know You are bringing."

Sustaining overflow requires humility. Pride stops the flow because it claims credit for what only grace could do. Humility keeps you teachable, pliable, and sensitive to the Spirit's guidance. When your heart remains humble in success, you become unstoppable in impact. Wealth without humility leads to spiritual bankruptcy. The truly rich are those who understand that everything they have belongs to God. They hold it lightly, they share it freely, and they manage it wisely. Humility turns possession into purpose.

Overflow also requires discernment. Not every opportunity is divine. Not every door is meant to be opened. Abundance will attract attention, but discernment protects direction. You must learn to say no to good things so you can say yes to God things.

Discernment helps you distinguish between distraction and destiny. It helps you recognise when something is meant to stretch you and when it is meant to drain you. Divine increase is sustainable only when it flows within divine boundaries.

Living in overflow also means learning to rest. Rest is not idleness; it is trust. It is the act of saying, "God, I have done my part, now I trust You with the rest." Rest is the rhythm of reliance. It keeps you from turning productivity into pride.

Without rest, increase becomes exhaustion. Without peace, prosperity becomes pressure. The Sabbath principle still applies today, not as a ritual, but as a reminder. Rest is an act of faith. It declares that you believe God will sustain what He started.

Divine Wealth

When you rest in Him, you stop striving for more and start receiving with ease. Grace begins to carry the weight that effort once held. You no longer work for blessing; you work from blessing. You are no longer chasing provision; you are walking with the Provider.

Overflow manifests when your spirit aligns with heaven's rhythm. It is not about trying harder, but about trusting deeper. The more you trust, the more you receive. The more you release, the lighter you become.

The anointing of increase is generational. What God gives you is never meant to stop with you. It is meant to outlive you. You are not just called to make wealth; you are called to make legacy. A legacy of faith, wisdom, generosity, and transformation.

Your overflow should bless your children, your community, your church, and your world. Legacy is not what you leave behind; it is who you leave empowered. It is the people you lift, the lives you change, and the seeds you plant in hearts that will never forget your impact.

Divine increase builds generational stability. When you teach your children how to honour God with wealth, you create a lineage of stewardship. When you train them to give, to serve, and to build, you leave them not just inheritance, but identity.

True prosperity is generational impact. It is seeing your blessings multiplied through others. It is watching your seed become a forest of future faith.

God's increase is never random. It is always redemptive. He blesses you to heal what was broken, to rebuild what was destroyed, and to restore what was lost. Your overflow is meant to correct the imbalance of lack in the world.

When the Church walks in the anointing of increase, poverty begins to lose its power. When believers become builders, nations begin to change. Wealth is not worldly when it is used for Kingdom purposes. It becomes worship when it lifts others higher.

Divine Wealth

Your generosity is a sermon. Your stewardship is your ministry. Every act of giving preaches the gospel louder than words. Every business built on godly principles becomes a pulpit of impact. Every job created in righteousness becomes a testimony of divine wisdom. The anointing of increase is not about chasing riches; it is about carrying responsibility. It is not about possession; it is about purpose. It is not about what you can get; it is about what you can give. When your increase becomes a form of worship, your wealth becomes holy. The more you use it to serve, the more sacred it becomes. Money, in the hands of the righteous, becomes a tool of transformation.

The ultimate purpose of increase is worship. Not the kind that happens in song, but the kind that happens in stewardship. It is the way you honour God with your time, your talent, and your treasure. It is the way you turn profit into purpose, success into service, and gain into glory.

When you live in overflow, every transaction becomes an offering. Every business deal becomes a ministry moment. Every seed sown becomes an act of faith. You stop separating the sacred and the secular because you realise that everything you touch can carry divine purpose.

Overflow is not for display; it is for destiny. God's intention is not that you become rich to boast, but that you become rich to build. You are not called to collect wealth; you are called to create impact. Your life becomes a vessel of generosity, a channel of provision, and a testimony of divine grace. You become the evidence that prosperity and purity can coexist, that faith and finance can walk hand in hand, that increase and integrity can grow together.

When you walk in this revelation, you begin to attract the right partnerships, opportunities, and assignments. Divine connections form around divine intentions. The same Spirit that anoints you for increase also guides you in its administration.

Divine Wealth

God's abundance will always flow toward His purpose. When you commit to His mission, you will never lack provision. When you build for His Kingdom, you will never struggle for resources. The anointing of increase carries its own supply.

Overflow is not an achievement; it is a trust. God trusts those who understand that wealth is sacred. He releases abundance to those who will protect its purpose.

When you live in overflow, you become a reflection of God's generosity. You radiate His goodness through every area of your life. Your peace becomes contagious. Your faith becomes inspiring. Your giving becomes transformative.

The world does not need more rich people; it needs more righteous ones. Those who understand that prosperity without purpose is emptiness, but prosperity with purpose is eternity.

You were never meant to fear wealth. You were meant to steward it. You were meant to use it as a weapon against injustice, as a shield for the weak, as a seed for the future.

Every resource God gives you is an invitation to represent Him. You become His ambassador in the marketplace, His voice in the boardroom, His hands in the community. You demonstrate that divine abundance is not selfishness; it is service.

Overflow is holy. It is the manifestation of God's heart on earth. It is heaven's generosity expressed through human hands. When the world sees believers prospering with humility, giving with joy, and leading with love, they will see the true nature of God revealed.

You are not just called to live blessed; you are called to live as a blessing. You are not just called to receive; you are called to release. You are not just called to prosper; you are called to transform.

The anointing of increase is the divine permission to do more, give more, and be more for the glory of God. It is the evidence that faith still multiplies, that obedience still opens heaven, that generosity still breaks chains.

Divine Wealth

When you live in overflow, you do not just experience prosperity; you embody purpose. You become a walking river of blessing, a moving miracle of grace, a living testimony of divine abundance. Overflow is not the end; it is the beginning of a greater story. It is the start of a life that points every blessing back to the One who gave it. It is the place where your purpose and prosperity finally become one.

Divine Wealth

Chapter 8: The Faith to Build: Constructing Wealth Through Vision, Work, and Worship

Divine Wealth

Every great move of God begins with a vision. It starts as a whisper in the spirit, a spark that ignites in the unseen before it becomes structure in the visible. Vision is the birthplace of destiny, the first sign that heaven has chosen to create something through you. When God gives vision, He also provides provision, but between the promise and the provision lies a sacred process called building. Building is the act of faith made tangible. It is where belief becomes bricks and dreams become foundations. It is the place where prayer meets planning and where spiritual conviction meets physical creation. Building requires faith, but it also requires work. It demands courage, focus, and perseverance, for faith without works remains incomplete.

The faith to build is not passive; it is active obedience. It moves even when the outcome is unclear. It trusts even when the evidence is invisible. Every builder in Scripture, from Noah to Nehemiah, carried a vision that seemed impossible. Yet their faith did not depend on what they could see; it depended on who had spoken.

Noah built the ark when there was no rain. Abraham built altars before he saw nations. Moses built a tabernacle in a desert where no one imagined abundance could dwell. Nehemiah rebuilt broken walls with nothing but faith and determination. Each one built not because conditions were perfect, but because conviction was powerful.

Faith is the architect, but obedience is the builder. Vision sketches the plan, but action lays the stones. Many believers receive the vision yet hesitate to build. They wait for certainty before starting, forgetting that faith is the certainty of what is unseen. The moment you act on divine instruction, heaven begins to supply what you need.

To build with God is to participate in creation itself. You become a vessel of divine expression, a living testimony that heaven still collaborates with earth. Faith is not merely believing that God can do it; it is believing that He can do it through you.

Divine Wealth

Every act of faith is an act of creation. Every step of obedience draws the unseen into the seen. The builder's hands become an extension of heaven's design. When you build in faith, your work becomes worship. Every blueprint, every plan, every sacrifice becomes a prayer in motion.

God is a builder. From the foundations of the world to the fabric of human destiny, His nature is creative. When you build, you reflect His likeness. You are most like God when you create, when you take what is raw and shape it into something purposeful, something beautiful, something eternal.

The faith to build begins with belief, but it is sustained by consistency. You cannot construct greatness on moments of inspiration alone; it must rest on habits of faithfulness. The walls of destiny are not built in a day. They rise stone by stone, prayer by prayer, act by act.

Every structure that endures is built on a foundation of patience. The world rushes, but heaven builds. The world celebrates quick results, but God celebrates steady faith. The tower built in haste will crumble in time, but the house built on obedience will stand against every storm.

Faith is the cement that binds purpose to perseverance. When discouragement comes, faith holds the structure together. When opposition rises, faith anchors the vision in place. Building requires not only skill but also spiritual stamina.

There will be seasons when you feel like nothing is progressing. You may pour your time, your strength, and your resources into the vision and see no fruit. In those moments, faith must take the lead. You are not building for applause; you are building for alignment. You are not building to be seen; you are building to be significant.

The early stages of any divine project are quiet. The foundation season is hidden, unseen by the world, but watched by heaven. God

Divine Wealth

tests the builder before He blesses the blueprint. He ensures that your heart is stable before your structure rises.

You cannot build divine things with divided motives. God blesses purity of purpose. When the foundation of your work is obedience, the outcome is always abundance. The builder's heart must be as strong as his hands.

Faithful builders understand that setbacks are not signs of failure; they are confirmations of progress. Every obstacle reveals what must be strengthened. Every delay refines what must be redefined. When you face resistance, it means you are constructing something that threatens darkness. The enemy only fights what carries eternal impact.

To build is to battle. Faith builders must fight doubt, fear, and discouragement. They must resist the temptation to compare their progress to others. Comparison is a thief that steals confidence and peace. Every structure has its own timeline, every vision its own pace. When you stay faithful to your season, you will see the beauty of your completion.

God's blueprint for your life is not generic; it is divine. It was written long before you took your first breath. The faith to build is the courage to follow that blueprint even when others do not understand it. You may be called to construct something that has never been seen before. That is the mark of divine originality.

The faith to build is also the faith to begin. Many never build because they never start. They keep waiting for the right moment, forgetting that the right moment begins when obedience begins. You do not need all the resources; you need the right revelation. When you start moving, heaven starts multiplying.

Building requires both vision and precision. Faith gives you the why, wisdom gives you the how. God provides vision, but He expects you to develop strategy. Planning is not unbelief; it is stewardship. The

Divine Wealth

same God who gives spiritual revelation also honours practical preparation.

Faith and wisdom walk hand in hand. Faith ignites passion, and wisdom directs it. Faith begins the work, and wisdom sustains it. The builder who prays without planning lacks balance, but the one who plans without praying lacks power. Divine success requires both.

The faith to build also involves partnership. No divine project is meant to be built alone. Even Jesus chose twelve to build with Him. God sends people who carry pieces of the plan you cannot see. Your vision needs collaboration, not isolation.

Partnership is the soil where increase grows. When you align with the right people, purpose accelerates. But partnerships must be discerned. Not everyone who admires your vision is meant to build beside you. Some are spectators; others are scaffolds. Scaffolds are useful for a time but not meant to stay when the structure is complete.

Learn to recognise divine builders. They do not compete; they complement. They do not drain; they develop. They carry tools, not jealousy. They share the weight, not the spotlight.

The faith to build also includes the faith to rebuild. Sometimes life breaks what you have built. Dreams collapse, plans fall apart, and progress seems lost. But faith rebuilds stronger. The hands that once trembled with fear become the hands that shape again with wisdom.

Rebuilding requires resilience. It demands forgiveness, humility, and perseverance. You must forgive yourself for the seasons that failed and trust that what was broken can be rebuilt in beauty. God specialises in restoration. What He rebuilds, He fortifies. What He restores, He multiplies.

The faith to build is not only about physical creation; it is about spiritual construction. It is about building inner strength, building trust, building character, and building communion with God. You cannot construct something divine outwardly without being

Divine Wealth

constructed inwardly. God builds the builder before He builds the blessing.

Every divine builder must learn to rest in the process. Do not despise small beginnings. Foundations may not be glamorous, but they are essential. The taller the structure, the deeper the base must go. God builds deep before He builds high.

In the early stages, it may feel like your work is buried in obscurity, but buried things are not forgotten. Seeds are buried before they bloom. What feels hidden is often being prepared.

Faith sees the invisible; patience builds the impossible. The combination of both brings the miracle into reality.

When you build with faith, you begin to experience divine partnership in motion. The Spirit becomes your architect, whispering direction when confusion clouds your vision. He gives clarity in chaos and strength in weakness. You learn to depend on divine direction more than human approval.

Building by faith means trusting that even when resources seem limited, God will provide. Provision follows purpose. The God who gives vision also funds vision. The same hands that placed the idea in your heart will place the resources in your path.

When you build for God, you build differently. You measure success by obedience, not by numbers. You celebrate faithfulness more than fame. You understand that what matters is not how fast you build, but how faithfully you build.

The faith to build transforms work into worship. Every meeting, every transaction, every plan becomes a sacred offering. Your labour becomes liturgy, your results become praise.

There is no such thing as secular work when it is surrendered to a sacred purpose. The carpenter's workshop can be a sanctuary, the office desk can be an altar, the business deal can be a testimony. When you dedicate your work to God, every result becomes a revelation of His goodness.

Divine Wealth

Work was never a curse; it was a calling. Before the fall, God gave Adam work. He placed him in the garden to tend and cultivate it. Work is the expression of divine creativity within human form. The anointing to build is part of the image of God in man.

When work becomes worship, prosperity becomes purpose. Wealth becomes ministry. Success becomes testimony. You begin to build not for validation, but for vocation. You realise that building is not about becoming rich, but about becoming relevant in the Kingdom.

Every great builder must learn to finish. The foundation may require faith, but the finish requires endurance. It is one thing to begin with excitement; it is another to persist with excellence. Many start with fire, but few sustain the flame. To complete what God begins in you, you must walk with both persistence and peace.

Completion is a divine attribute. God never begins what He does not intend to finish. When He created the world, He completed it and then rested. His rest was not exhaustion; it was satisfaction. The faith to build includes the faith to complete, for every builder carries within them a reflection of God's creative nature.

You are not called to half-built dreams or unfinished visions. Heaven's blueprint is full and perfect, and the Spirit within you compels completion. The same grace that started the work will empower you to finish it. What God authors, He also anoints to completion.

There is a sacred satisfaction in finishing well. It is not pride; it is purpose fulfilled. It is the moment when obedience meets outcome and when effort transforms into evidence. The builder who completes the vision experiences the joy of divine alignment, the peace of knowing that nothing was wasted, and the honour of offering the finished work back to God.

Every phase of building reveals a new aspect of faith. The foundation tests your patience. The walls test your perseverance. The roof tests your vision. But the finishing work tests your excellence. Excellence

Divine Wealth

is the final expression of faithfulness. It says, "If this is for God, it must reflect His glory."

Excellence is not perfection; it is devotion. It is the commitment to give your best, not because people demand it, but because God deserves it. Excellence turns ordinary work into extraordinary worship. When you build with excellence, you declare that mediocrity has no place in the Kingdom.

The world often measures success by scale, but heaven measures it by sincerity. God does not reward how much you build, but how purely you build. The smallest act done with excellence carries greater weight in eternity than the grandest project done without integrity.

Building requires endurance because greatness is not created in comfort. Every wall that stands strong has faced pressure. Every pillar that holds weight has been tested. God allows pressure to prove the strength of your foundation. Pressure is not punishment; it is preparation.

The storms of life do not come to destroy the structure; they come to reveal its strength. When the winds blow and the rains fall, the builder who stands firm on faith cannot be shaken. Storms refine stability. They teach the builder to depend on the strength of God rather than the stability of circumstances.

Faith is the architect of resilience. When fatigue sets in and progress seems slow, faith whispers, "Keep building." When resources run low, faith says, "Provision is coming." When critics speak, faith responds, "My approval comes from heaven." Every great builder learns to listen to faith's voice above all others.

There will be times when God calls you to build in obscurity. These are the quiet seasons when no one sees your effort, when no one praises your progress. Yet it is in these seasons that your strength is forged. The absence of recognition is often the presence of refinement. God builds endurance in the shadows so that your light can stand firm in the spotlight.

Divine Wealth

The faith to build also includes the grace to pause. Rest is not quitting; it is recalibrating. Builders who never rest begin to break. The body tires, but so does the soul. God Himself instituted rest as part of the rhythm of creation. He knew that even holy work needs holy pauses.

When you rest, you allow God to refresh your vision. Clarity often comes in stillness. In the silence of rest, the next instruction becomes clear. Builders who neglect rest lose sensitivity to divine direction. The Spirit of God often speaks in whispers, and whispers require quiet. To hear the next phase, you must quiet the noise of overwork and ambition. The faith to build includes the humility to step back and listen.

When you build in partnership with heaven, your structure becomes eternal. It carries within it the breath of the Spirit. Buildings made of stone may crumble, but structures built on faith remain forever. Every soul you touch, every life you uplift, every act of obedience becomes part of your eternal architecture.

Your legacy is not just what you build; it is who you build. The greatest projects in the Kingdom are not monuments of metal or glass; they are people. The disciples Jesus built changed the world because they carried His design within them. When you invest in others, you multiply your purpose beyond your lifetime.

To build people is the highest form of building. It is to see potential where others see imperfection. It is to speak life into gifts that have not yet awakened. It is to nurture greatness until it begins to rise. The faith to build others requires patience, love, and vision. It means believing in people before they believe in themselves.

When you build people, you build perpetuity. Your influence becomes generational. Your wisdom becomes seed for future builders. The legacy of faith is not wealth left behind, but wisdom passed on.

Divine Wealth

Divine builders understand that wealth is a by-product of work, but legacy is the purpose of it. God blesses you not just to increase your possessions, but to extend your influence. The greater your impact, the greater your responsibility.

The faith to build also demands that you manage what you have built. Many lose what they have because they neglect what they own. Stewardship does not end when the structure stands; it continues in the care that follows. Maintenance is the proof of maturity.

God honours the builder who protects what has been built. Neglect invites decay. Diligence invites durability. To sustain divine increase, you must nurture what has already been entrusted to you.

The Spirit of wisdom teaches how to manage overflow. It reminds you that resources are not only for enjoyment but for empowerment. Wealth managed well becomes a tool of transformation. When you sustain what God has given, you qualify for more.

Every builder reaches a point where expansion becomes necessary. Growth requires courage. To expand means to stretch. The same faith that began the work must now believe for greater capacity. You cannot contain new vision within old vessels. You must be willing to upgrade your systems, your thinking, and your strategies.

God will never give you more than your current structure can hold. When you feel limited, it is a sign to enlarge your capacity. Increase always begins internally before it manifests externally.

The faith to build becomes the faith to expand. You cannot be content with past success when future purpose is calling. The builder who stops growing stops building. Vision must evolve; faith must increase.

Excellence also requires evaluation. Every divine builder must pause to assess progress. Reflection refines direction. To evaluate is not to doubt; it is to strengthen. God gives revelation through reflection. When you look back in gratitude, you find guidance for what is next.

Divine Wealth

To build well is to build for eternity. You are not just constructing wealth for your generation; you are creating foundations for generations yet unborn. Your faith today builds stability for the future.

The world may measure success by what you accumulate, but heaven measures it by what you activate. What did your faith unlock? Whose destiny did your obedience awaken? What eternal difference did your vision make? These are the questions that define divine achievement. The faith to build is not only about doing; it is about becoming.

Every act of obedience shapes you into a vessel of divine excellence. As you build outwardly, God builds inwardly. He forms patience in your waiting, humility in your leading, and strength in your serving. Every brick of obedience forms the cathedral of character. Every stone of surrender becomes part of the temple of trust. By the time the vision is complete, you are no longer who you were when you began. You have become stronger, wiser, and more surrendered. Building is not just about constructing something for God; it is about allowing God to construct something in you. The structure outside is temporary, but the structure within is eternal.

When you reach the moment of completion, lift your eyes and give glory where it belongs. The finished work is not your achievement; it is your offering. The true builder knows that without the Master Architect, no blueprint could have become reality.

To dedicate what you have built is to release it back to the One who made it possible. It is to say, "Lord, this belongs to You. Use it for Your glory." That is when the work becomes worship, when effort becomes eternal, when faith finds fulfillment.

You will know you have built well when your work outlives your name. When your influence continues after your hands have rested. When your obedience becomes the foundation for others to build upon.

Divine Wealth

God is raising builders for this generation , men and women who will construct systems of justice, temples of transformation, and networks of generosity. Builders who will carry the torch of divine creativity into every field, from business to art, from education to governance. Builders who will prove that faith still builds, and that God still breathes through human hands.

The call to build is not for the faint-hearted, but for the faithful. It is a call to courage, endurance, and devotion. It is a call to take vision and turn it into value, to take revelation and turn it into reality. It is the invitation to become an instrument through which heaven shapes earth.

If you are called to build, know that you are not alone. The same Spirit that hovered over the waters in Genesis hovers over your plans today. The same breath that brought order to chaos breathes into your vision. You are building with God, not for Him.

When the final stone is laid and the work stands complete, may your heart echo the words of Christ: "It is finished." Not because you have nothing left to do, but because you have done what He asked. That is the greatest success a builder can know.

Divine Wealth

Chapter 9: Harvest of the Heart, Reaping God's Abundance Through Generosity and Grace

Divine Wealth

There is a rhythm in the Kingdom that never fails, a divine pattern that governs both heaven and earth. It is the rhythm of giving and receiving, the eternal law of sowing and reaping. Every seed carries within it a promise, and every act of generosity sets that promise into motion. The soil of the heart is where abundance begins, and what you release determines what will return to you.

True wealth begins in the heart, not in the hands. Before there is a harvest, there must be a seed, and before there is a seed, there must be surrender. Generosity is not measured by how much you give, but by how freely you give. It is the act of letting go that opens the door for heaven to pour in.

God designed the universe to respond to release. When you hold tightly, nothing flows, but when you open your hands, heaven recognises faith. Faith is always expressed through action, and giving is one of faith's purest expressions. When you give, you declare, "My source is not what I have, my source is who I serve."

The soil of generosity is sacred. Every act of kindness, every offering, every moment of compassion is a seed planted in eternity. You may not always see the harvest immediately, but heaven keeps record. The God who sees in secret rewards in ways that exceed imagination.

In every age and every culture, those who live with open hearts rise above scarcity. They are not trapped by fear, for they have learned that supply is sustained by surrender. Scarcity begins where gratitude ends, and abundance begins where generosity lives.

The principle of sowing and reaping is not a formula, it is a relationship. It is the divine partnership between Creator and creation. When you give, you are not losing, you are aligning. You are synchronising your spirit with heaven's flow.

Money is not the master of this law, love is. Generosity is the language of love in action. It is the way faith becomes visible. Every seed you plant carries the fingerprint of your faith and the fragrance

Divine Wealth

of your intention. If you give grudgingly, the soil resists. If you give freely, the ground rejoices.

The generous heart does not give because it must, it gives because it trusts. It knows that no gift given in love ever truly leaves your life, it simply changes form. It leaves your hand but never leaves your future. What you release in obedience returns in overflow.

When a farmer sows seed, he does not cry over the soil. He understands that what leaves his hand today will rise again tomorrow in multiplied form. Faith is the same. You give not because of loss, but because of expectation. You give knowing that your seed has an assignment.

Generosity is not limited to money. It is a way of living. It is found in words that uplift, in time shared with the weary, in kindness shown when no one is watching. Every act of goodness is an investment in eternity.

When you live generously, you create an atmosphere that attracts divine attention. Heaven responds to hearts that reflect its nature. God Himself is the greatest giver, for He so loved the world that He gave His Son. To give is to resemble God. To withhold is to resist His likeness.

There is a spiritual maturity that comes from generosity. It refines the soul and releases joy. The tight-fisted heart lives in fear, but the open hand lives in faith. Fear says, "If I give, I will lose." Faith says, "If I give, I will grow."

The secret of increase lies in understanding that God never multiplies what you keep, He multiplies what you sow. The seed that remains in your pocket is safe, but sterile. The seed that touches the soil is vulnerable, but fruitful. You must be willing to let go to receive more. This truth applies not only to wealth but to wisdom, opportunity, and influence. The more you share, the more you expand. Holding knowledge for yourself limits its impact, but sharing it multiplies revelation. The law of sowing governs every form of abundance.

Divine Wealth

Some believers misunderstand this principle, thinking that giving is merely an exchange, something done to get something in return. But true giving is not transactional, it is transformational. The transformation happens first within you, as giving stretches your faith and strengthens your trust. Then, in due season, it manifests outwardly as blessing and increase.

The posture of a generous heart is gratitude. Gratitude unlocks giving, and giving unlocks growth. A thankful person never runs out of reasons to give, because they recognise that everything they have is grace. When you live from gratitude, giving is no longer a sacrifice, it is a celebration.

Giving shifts your focus from what you lack to what you already possess. It transforms scarcity into sufficiency and sufficiency into abundance. Gratitude expands perception. It allows you to see God's provision even in small beginnings.

When you give, you participate in God's ecosystem of abundance. You become a conduit of blessing. The river that refuses to flow becomes stagnant, but the river that flows freely remains full. The more you allow blessings to pass through you, the more heaven entrusts to you.

Generosity is a sign of spiritual maturity because it requires trust. You cannot be generous if you do not trust the Giver. The more you know God's character, the more freely you can give. You begin to understand that your provision is secure in His promise.

To give is to exercise faith over fear, trust over tension, love over lack. It is to live by revelation, not by reaction. It is to say, "I will not be moved by what I see, but by what I believe."

When you give with joy, you multiply joy. When you give with love, you multiply love. The heart that releases blessing becomes the vessel through which blessing continues to flow.

Even in times of lack, giving opens doors. The widow of Zarephath gave her last meal to Elijah, and her jar of oil never ran dry. The boy

Divine Wealth

with five loaves and two fish gave what seemed insignificant, and God used it to feed thousands. In both stories, lack became abundance because generosity met obedience.

The size of the gift never matters to God, the spirit behind it does. Heaven measures not by quantity, but by quality of faith. A seed may look small, but when sown in faith, it carries exponential potential. Every time you give, you are writing a testimony. Every time you release, you are declaring that your faith is greater than your fear. Each act of generosity plants hope into the soil of humanity.

The harvest of the heart is not only material, it is emotional and spiritual. Generosity heals bitterness, breaks pride, and restores peace. It turns self-focus into compassion, comparison into contentment, and fear into freedom.

When you give, you become part of a divine transaction that no earthly economy can measure. Heaven calculates differently. It counts the intention, not the amount.

Giving also aligns you with divine timing. Some doors open only when generosity precedes them. When you give into purpose, you activate provision. Many prayers for breakthrough are answered through acts of release.

The key to sustained abundance is consistency. Habits of generosity shape your heart and reveal your trust in God. Each act of giving reinforces who you are, a child of a generous Father. The more you practice generosity, the more natural it becomes.

To live in the rhythm of sowing and reaping is to live in harmony with heaven. It is to flow with the seasons of giving and harvest, trusting that the God who brings rain to the earth will bring increase to your seed.

When you plant seeds of love, joy, wisdom, and resources, you prepare the ground for miracles. Your seed may leave your hand today, but it will never leave your life. It will reappear in ways you

Divine Wealth

never expected, through open doors, restored relationships, unexpected provision, or renewed strength.
The harvest of the heart is certain, because the Giver is faithful. Heaven never forgets a seed sown in love.
Generosity does not end when the giving is done, it begins anew each time the heart opens. The cycle of giving and receiving is continuous, like the rising of the sun and the rhythm of the tide. To give once is an act of kindness, but to live in generosity is a state of grace. The generous heart learns that every harvest is simply another opportunity to plant again.
Sustained abundance is not built on single acts, but on consistent habits of trust. When giving becomes a rhythm instead of an occasion, the heart becomes a vessel that heaven can rely on. God does not only bless those who give, He blesses those who can be trusted to keep the flow open. The hands that release with joy will never remain empty for long.
The discipline of generosity transforms the giver more than the receiver. Every time you give, a layer of fear falls away. Every time you release, your faith grows stronger. Every offering teaches the soul to trust that God's provision never runs out. The more you give, the more you realise that abundance was never about possessions, it was always about perspective.
Abundance is not measured by what you hold, but by what you release. The river does not stay full because it hoards the water, but because it keeps it moving. When you live with open hands, you live in partnership with divine flow. When you stop giving, you stop growing.
To sustain a lifestyle of generosity, you must first cultivate a heart of contentment. Contentment protects generosity from greed. It reminds you that giving is not a competition, it is communion. You do not give to impress others, you give to express faith.

Divine Wealth

Contentment does not mean complacency. It does not tell you to stop dreaming, it teaches you to dream without desperation. It allows you to pursue increase without losing peace. The content heart can give without fear because it has learned to rest in the goodness of God.

When you are content, you can handle abundance without arrogance and manage lack without despair. You understand that your worth does not rise or fall with your wealth. You are anchored in identity, not inventory. This is the secret of those who live blessed and unbothered.

To sustain your harvest, you must remain rooted in purpose. Purpose gives direction to prosperity. Without it, abundance becomes a burden. Wealth without purpose leads to confusion, but wealth with purpose leads to creation. God blesses with intention. When your increase aligns with His purpose, your provision never ends.

Every resource has an assignment. Every blessing carries a purpose beyond pleasure. God does not give randomly, He gives strategically. When He finds a heart that can channel His blessings toward others, He multiplies that flow. Heaven expands through hearts that give freely.

To keep the harvest alive, you must guard your motives. Give because you love, not because you lack. Give because you trust, not because you fear. Give because you want to reflect the heart of God, not because you want to impress the world. Purity of motive keeps your giving sacred.

When giving becomes performance, it loses power. When it becomes worship, it carries weight. The most powerful gifts are not the largest ones, but the purest ones. The quiet giver, unseen by crowds but known by heaven, moves God's heart more than a thousand public displays.

True generosity is silent, steady, and sincere. It is done from a heart that understands that to give is to breathe, to bless is to live. It is a

Divine Wealth

spiritual reflex, not a social performance. Heaven does not need applause to release reward.

Sustaining generosity also requires discernment. Giving without wisdom can drain rather than bless. There are moments when God calls you to sow into specific soil, to invest where His Spirit leads. Not every need is your assignment. The key is to listen for divine instruction before releasing your seed.

The greatest givers are also great listeners. They give where heaven directs. They understand that obedience magnifies outcome. A seed planted in the wrong soil struggles to grow, but one planted in divine purpose produces beyond imagination.

To maintain divine flow, you must live with both open hands and an open heart. The hand releases, but the heart receives. The same faith that gives must also learn to receive. Many believers find it easier to give than to receive, but both are part of the same spiritual equation. Giving without receiving breaks balance.

Receiving is not selfishness; it is stewardship. It is saying to God, "I am ready to manage what You entrust." When you receive with gratitude, you honour the Giver. The cycle continues, and abundance multiplies again.

God desires for His children to be both givers and receivers, to both bless and be blessed, to both sow and harvest. The cycle of generosity reflects His nature. He gives, and He delights in seeing His children give in return.

The harvest you sustain through generosity becomes the foundation of your legacy. Legacy is what happens when generosity outlives the giver. It is when your giving becomes a story that continues after you are gone. Every life you touch, every soul you lift, every opportunity you create becomes part of that living story.

Legacy is not built in a day; it is built in daily decisions. Each act of kindness becomes a brick in the monument of your impact. Each sacrifice becomes a seed that future generations will harvest.

Divine Wealth

When you give, you are not only shaping your present; you are sculpting eternity. The fruit of your generosity will feed people you may never meet. It will inspire hearts you may never know. That is the power of divine giving, it multiplies beyond your reach.

The most powerful legacies are not written in numbers, they are written in names, in lives, in stories. The businesses started, the scholarships funded, the churches built, the families restored, these are the true measures of prosperity.

Generosity does not erase challenges, but it transforms them. When storms come, the generous soul remains secure because their confidence was never in their possessions. They know that what was sown in faith cannot be stolen by fear.

The generous believer is unshaken by economic tides, because their wealth is rooted in spiritual law. The systems of earth may rise and fall, but the system of sowing and reaping remains eternal. The markets of man fluctuate, but the harvest of heaven is constant.

When you live in divine generosity, you become unmovable. You understand that what is planted in obedience cannot fail, because the One who watches over the seed is faithful. You may not control the weather, but you can always control what you sow.

Generosity is also contagious. When one heart begins to give, it inspires another. The light of one generous act can ignite entire communities. Giving spreads hope like fire, burning through despair and darkness until joy rises again.

In every generation, God raises givers to break cycles of lack. He uses those who live with open hearts to release blessings that transform nations. Generosity is not limited by wealth, it is measured by willingness. God can use anyone who says, "Yes, Lord, use what I have."

Your giving might seem small in the world's eyes, but in God's economy, it is priceless. Heaven counts differently. The gift that changes one life has already changed eternity.

Divine Wealth

When you give, you join the divine work of creation. You take part in restoring what has been broken and reviving what has been lost. Giving is redemption in motion. It turns sorrow into song and lack into life.

There will always be moments when the enemy whispers, "What you give will be wasted." But faith replies, "Nothing given in love is ever lost." Every seed, every prayer, every sacrifice, carries eternal weight. Heaven sees, heaven remembers, and heaven multiplies.

When you live in this truth, you stop fearing loss. You begin to see that your life itself is a seed. You were created to give, to serve, to bless. When you live as a seed, you will always produce fruit.

To live generously is to live freely. To give is to declare that no possession holds your heart. It is to walk in victory over greed, to rise above fear, and to dwell in divine trust. The generous life is the joyful life, for the one who gives continually walks in communion with heaven's heartbeat.

Generosity is worship in motion. It is prayer made visible. It is love dressed in action. When you give, you become a reflection of divine nature, a mirror of God's mercy.

The harvest of your life will not be counted in wealth, but in wonder. It will be measured by the joy you released, the hope you ignited, the faith you strengthened, and the love you gave.

And when your work on earth is done, may heaven greet you with the words, "Well done, good and faithful servant, you gave with love, you lived with purpose, you reflected the heart of your Father."

This is the reward of the generous, the joy of those who understood that abundance is not what you keep, but what you release. The harvest of the heart never ends, for love always multiplies.

Divine Wealth

Chapter 10: The Anointing of Increase, Walking in Divine Prosperity Without Losing Your Purpose

Divine Wealth

Increase is not a coincidence, it is a calling. It is not a random outcome, it is a divine endorsement. When God blesses you with more, He is not only enlarging your possession, He is expanding your purpose. Prosperity in the Kingdom is not for prestige, it is for purpose. It is the equipping of the believer to do greater works, to build, to serve, to bless, and to reveal the heart of the Father through abundance.

Every good thing begins in seed form, yet when God breathes upon it, it multiplies beyond measure. The anointing of increase is the mark of divine favour resting upon your effort, transforming ordinary work into extraordinary impact. It is the invisible empowerment that takes human hands and turns them into instruments of heaven's abundance.

But divine increase is not random. God does not anoint every vessel for wealth, He anoints those who are ready to carry it with integrity. The increase of God is not simply given; it is trusted. Heaven measures the weight of the heart before it multiplies the work of the hands.

If your heart is ready, your harvest is near. If your motive is pure, your miracle is already forming. God tests the steward before He releases the storehouse. The measure of faithfulness in small things determines the capacity to manage great ones.

The anointing of increase comes to those who are willing to serve, not those who seek status. Prosperity is not a crown; it is a commission. When you receive divine abundance, you are receiving responsibility. Heaven entrusts wealth to those who will distribute it in alignment with God's will.

True prosperity is not the goal; it is the outcome of obedience. You do not chase wealth; you chase wisdom, and wealth follows. The same God who gave Solomon riches beyond imagination gave him wisdom first. When your heart seeks understanding more than

Divine Wealth

accumulation, God ensures that both wisdom and wealth dwell within you.

The danger is not in increase itself, but in forgetting the purpose of it. Many lose their way when blessing becomes the focus instead of the fruit of obedience. The purpose of prosperity is not to elevate self, but to empower service. The hands that receive must remain open so that others may be blessed through them.

Increase without intimacy leads to emptiness. When the gift grows greater than the Giver, the heart becomes hollow. That is why divine prosperity must always be anchored in worship. Every blessing must return to the altar, every success must bow before the Source.

The anointing of increase is the empowerment to expand without losing your essence. It allows you to carry more while remaining humble, to influence many while staying grounded, to lead with love rather than pride. True abundance does not corrupt; it consecrates. It draws you closer to God because you recognise that every gift flows from Him.

God's design for prosperity is deeply relational. He increases what will glorify Him. When your prosperity points back to the Provider, it becomes worship in motion. The anointing of increase is not about numbers; it is about alignment. When you align your purpose with God's priorities, increase becomes inevitable.

The anointing of increase also requires capacity. God will not pour new wine into old wineskins. Before He multiplies what you have, He multiplies who you are. The vessel must be stretched before it can carry more. Growth always begins within. Expansion of influence begins with expansion of character.

When God prepares you for increase, He first transforms your mindset. Poverty is not only a lack of money; it is a lack of vision. The poor in spirit are not those without possessions, but those without purpose. When you begin to see wealth as a tool, not a trophy, you step into maturity.

Divine Wealth

The renewed mind sees abundance differently. It does not measure success by comparison, but by contribution. It does not chase recognition, it seeks revelation. When you understand that prosperity is partnership with God, you stop striving and start stewarding. You no longer pray, "Lord, make me rich," but "Lord, make me ready." The anointing of increase does not exempt you from challenges; it equips you to overcome them. Every promotion carries new pressure, but the same Spirit that brings increase also brings endurance. With every blessing comes a new battlefield, but those who are anointed to prosper are also anointed to persevere.

In the story of Joseph, we see the perfect picture of divine increase. Betrayed, enslaved, imprisoned, yet never forgotten by God. Every season of struggle was preparation for stewardship. When the time of increase came, Joseph did not use it for revenge; he used it for redemption. The same wisdom that preserved Egypt preserved his family. Prosperity became the platform for reconciliation.

Joseph's story reveals that increase is not only about elevation, it is about preservation. God raises some to rescue many. The wealth of the righteous is never just personal, it is purposeful.

Every anointed increase carries a mission. For some, it is to build; for others, to restore; for others still, to heal. The wealth that flows from heaven always carries a divine assignment. The more you understand your mission, the more clearly you will see why God has blessed you. You were never meant to chase money; you were meant to attract it through mastery, discipline, and divine alignment. When you walk in purpose, provision follows like a shadow. You do not need to manipulate opportunity; you magnetise it through obedience.

The anointing of increase is not for everyone who desires more; it is for those who are willing to manage more with reverence. To be trusted with abundance, you must first master restraint. To carry glory, you must first walk in humility.

Divine Wealth

Wealth without wisdom destroys, but wealth with worship multiplies. God's plan for His children is not poverty, but purpose. Poverty restricts; purpose releases. When you pursue purpose with passion, heaven releases provision with power.

To walk in divine prosperity, you must learn to separate possession from identity. What you have is not who you are. You are not defined by your bank account, but by your divine assignment. The richest person in the world can still be poor in peace, while the humble servant walking in obedience may possess treasures no money can buy.

The truly prosperous believer carries peace, joy, and purpose wherever they go. They understand that their worth is anchored in who they belong to, not what they own. Their wealth becomes a witness, their success a sermon, their prosperity a proclamation that God is faithful.

The anointing of increase is not seasonal; it is sustainable. It grows with you as you grow in grace. It deepens as your devotion deepens. It strengthens as your stewardship strengthens. You cannot outgive, outgrow, or outlast the God of increase.

Divine prosperity moves in cycles. It begins with obedience, flows through stewardship, multiplies through generosity, and returns in worship. When you live within that cycle, lack cannot linger. You may face trials, but you will not stay barren. Your source is not the economy of man, but the economy of heaven.

Every time you walk in faithfulness, you qualify for more. Every time you honour God with what you have, He entrusts you with greater. The anointing of increase responds to faith, not formula. Heaven's currency is obedience, and its interest is eternal.

When God increases you, He expects you to influence others. Prosperity is not meant to end with you, it is meant to extend through you. You are the continuation of God's generosity on earth. The hands of the believer are the hands through which heaven gives.

Divine Wealth

True prosperity is a bridge between heaven's abundance and earth's need. The more you carry, the more responsible you become. God does not bless you to boast; He blesses you to build. He enlarges your territory so that you may enlarge His Kingdom.

Increase should never isolate you; it should involve you. It should draw you deeper into community, compassion, and contribution. The truly blessed soul does not rise above others; it lifts others with it. The anointing of increase is a gift, but it is also a test. Every blessing reveals what truly rules the heart. Prosperity is not proof of superiority, it is proof of stewardship. It is not a medal of honour, it is a mantle of service. The true test of success is not how high you rise, but how deeply you remain rooted in God while you do.

If humility does not anchor your prosperity, pride will sabotage it. Pride is the silent thief that enters unnoticed. It whispers that what you have is the result of your own strength, your own wisdom, your own merit. But those who carry divine increase know that it was never their doing. They understand that grace opened the doors, faith walked through them, and obedience kept them open.

The anointing of increase cannot rest upon the proud, because pride blocks the flow of grace. God resists the proud but gives grace to the humble. Humility does not deny the blessing; it defines it correctly. It says, "Everything I have is a gift, and every gift is for His glory."

To sustain increase, gratitude must become your foundation. Gratitude keeps the soul grounded in truth. It reminds you that success is not entitlement; it is entrustment. Every time you pause to give thanks, you strengthen your connection to the Source. The grateful heart never runs dry, because thanksgiving attracts fresh outpouring.

Gratitude transforms the way you see abundance. It shifts your focus from accumulation to appreciation, from greed to grace. When you live in gratitude, every resource becomes sacred, every opportunity becomes holy, every achievement becomes worship.

Divine Wealth

Prosperity is safest in the hands of the thankful. The ungrateful eventually misuse what they receive, because they forget where it came from. But the one who remembers the Giver never mishandles the gift. Gratitude keeps increase from turning into idolatry.

You cannot serve two masters. Money makes a wonderful servant but a terrible master. When you love money, you lose peace; when you use money for purpose, you gain both peace and power. The anointing of increase is not about loving wealth, it is about loving God enough to handle wealth wisely.

To live in divine prosperity is to live in balance. It is the discipline of stewardship joined with the joy of abundance. It is learning to live well without living wastefully, to enjoy blessing without being enslaved by it. The anointed believer walks in freedom because they know how to master what they possess rather than being mastered by it.

Increase without direction becomes distraction. God never blesses you to keep you busy; He blesses you to keep you building. Every resource you receive must be assigned purpose. If you do not give your prosperity purpose, the world will give it one for you.

To sustain prosperity, vision must be clear. Without vision, abundance leaks. Wealth follows focus. The clearer your divine assignment, the more accurately your resources flow. The anointing of increase requires direction, discipline, and divine awareness.

You must learn to hear the rhythm of heaven even in seasons of abundance. Prosperity can be noisy. Success attracts many voices, but not every voice deserves your attention. The higher you rise, the more silent you must become before God. Stillness preserves clarity. Quietness keeps your discernment sharp.

In the midst of increase, guard your heart from arrogance and your ears from flattery. Flattery inflates the ego and blinds the spirit. People may praise the results, but only God knows the cost. Do not

Divine Wealth

allow applause to replace anointing. Let every compliment become a crown you lay back at the feet of Christ.

True greatness never forgets its dependence on grace. Every great man or woman of God who has carried increase with honour has done so through humility. The most anointed are always the most aware of their need for God. Their prosperity amplifies their praise, not their pride.

Divine prosperity is a circle, not a straight line. It begins in obedience, grows through stewardship, multiplies through generosity, and returns in worship. Each stage sustains the next. When one is neglected, the flow weakens. To remain fruitful, you must remain faithful in every stage.

The anointing of increase demands accountability. To whom much is given, much is required. The responsibility of wealth is not simply management; it is multiplication. God expects increase on what He entrusts. The parable of the talents is not about profit alone, it is about faithfulness. The servant who multiplied his portion was not praised for success, but for stewardship.

To sustain divine prosperity, you must be willing to partner with others. Increase is not meant to isolate you, it is meant to connect you. God's blessings often come with people attached, divine relationships that carry wisdom, protection, and partnership.

The anointing of increase thrives in community. Prosperity that blesses only one person fades, but prosperity that blesses a generation endures. Your increase should always have an "us" in it, never only "me."

You must also learn to rest in increase. Anxiety does not protect prosperity; it pollutes it. Fear of losing what you have can become as destructive as the lack you once feared. Peace is the guardian of true wealth. When you rest in God, you release the need to control outcomes.

Divine Wealth

To live in sustained prosperity, you must let go of striving. Striving is the symptom of disbelief. It says, "I must make it happen." Faith says, "God will establish it." The anointed believer does not hustle in panic, they move with peace. They know that divine timing governs divine increase.

The pace of prosperity in the Kingdom is not driven by competition; it is guided by conviction. Your success does not require someone else's failure. Heaven has no shortage of blessing. The same God who lifted you can lift others without diminishing your portion. When you celebrate the success of others, you enlarge your own capacity to receive.

Generosity keeps prosperity flowing, but so does celebration. Gratitude and joy multiply blessing. When you celebrate another person's breakthrough, you signal to heaven that you are ready for your own. Jealousy closes the door to increase, but joy keeps it wide open.

To walk in divine increase is to walk in light. It means shining so that others may find their path. You do not hide your blessings in shame or display them in pride; you carry them with purpose. Your prosperity is not meant to make others feel small; it is meant to make God look great.

The presence of prosperity in your life should lead people to the presence of God. When others see peace in your success, integrity in your influence, and compassion in your power, they will know that heaven is at work through you.

You sustain the anointing of increase by staying surrendered. The moment you believe that you own the blessing, it begins to own you. The moment you recognise that you are only a steward, it continues to flow through you. Surrender is not loss; it is leverage. It invites God to do more through you than you could ever do alone.

Surrender keeps your heart light. It frees you from fear, for what you give to God cannot be taken from you. The surrendered soul lives

Divine Wealth

without anxiety because they have nothing to lose and everything to gain. Their treasure is not stored on earth but in obedience.

God's anointing for increase is never about accumulation; it is about amplification. He multiplies what will magnify His name. He blesses what will bless others. He increases what will inspire worship. When you use your wealth to lift others, you join heaven's melody of mercy and generosity.

Sustaining prosperity also means being teachable. Wisdom keeps wealth alive. The moment you believe you know it all, you close yourself off from new revelation. Divine prosperity flows through humility, and humility always remains a student.

The truly prosperous are lifelong learners. They seek wisdom not to boast, but to serve. They read, listen, observe, and discern, because they know that one idea from God can change generations. Their minds are open, but their hearts are guarded by truth.

You cannot sustain the anointing of increase without discipline. Discipline is devotion in motion. It is how you protect what you have been given. The careless spend; the wise steward. The fearful hoard; the faithful multiply. Prosperity responds to principle. When you live by divine order, wealth finds stability in your hands.

Every believer must learn the rhythm of divine order. God's blessings flow best through structure. Chaos repels increase. Organisation is not worldly; it is spiritual. The same God who created the stars in precise alignment expects excellence in how you manage your resources.

The anointing of increase must be protected through prayer. Prayer keeps prosperity pure. It keeps the heart soft, the motive clear, and the spirit sensitive. Without prayer, prosperity becomes noise; with prayer, it becomes harmony.

When you pray over your business, your projects, your resources, you invite the Spirit of God to remain involved. Prayer consecrates

Divine Wealth

increase. It keeps success from becoming separation. The more God blesses you, the more you must pray.

The mature believer does not let prosperity distance them from God; they let it draw them closer. The greater the blessing, the deeper the bow. Every act of worship is a declaration that God is still the center of your success.

The anointing of increase grows stronger when it is shared. The most powerful wealth is collective wealth, the kind that empowers others to walk in their own purpose. When you use your influence to mentor, support, or lift others, your anointing expands. Heaven rewards what multiplies goodness.

To walk in divine prosperity is to live in gratitude, generosity, and grace. It is to embody the truth that wealth is not about what you possess, but about what you release. Prosperity is the echo of obedience, the reflection of divine favour, and the signature of stewardship.

In the end, the anointing of increase is not about success, it is about surrender. It is not about the accumulation of more, but the alignment of motive. It is not about the riches you hold, but the righteousness you reflect.

When you can lift your hands in worship at the height of your blessing just as easily as you did in your season of lack, you have passed the test of increase. That is when prosperity becomes peace. The anointing of increase is a sacred invitation. It calls you to live above fear, to lead with purpose, to give with joy, and to build with integrity. It is the blessing that proves God still trusts humanity to reveal His goodness on earth.

When you live in that truth, wealth becomes worship, work becomes witness, and prosperity becomes purpose fulfilled. You carry heaven's light wherever you go, not as a symbol of status, but as a sign of surrender. That is the highest form of abundance, and that is the true anointing of increase.

Divine Wealth

Divine Wealth

Chapter 11: The Covenant of Contentment, Finding Joy and Purpose in Every Season of Provision

Divine Wealth

There comes a point in every believer's journey where the pursuit of more must meet the peace of enough. True prosperity does not simply come from the increase in what we hold, but from the understanding of what already rests within our hands. The covenant of contentment is one of the greatest treasures in the Kingdom, for it anchors the heart when the storms of striving rage around it. Contentment is not complacency, it is clarity. It is the moment when your soul whispers, "God is enough, and in Him, I have all things." It is not the denial of desire, but the sanctification of it. Desire without contentment leads to exhaustion, but desire guided by peace leads to purpose.

The world teaches us to chase, but heaven teaches us to rest. The voice of the world says, "You are behind," but the voice of the Spirit says, "You are becoming." In the stillness of God's presence, the believer discovers that peace and prosperity are not opposites, they are partners. They coexist in the heart that trusts fully in the Provider. There is a holy rhythm in the life of the content soul. It moves from gratitude to grace, from peace to purpose, from stillness to strength. The content heart is not passive; it is powerful. It sees clearly, it hears deeply, and it acts wisely. It is not driven by comparison, but guided by conviction.

The covenant of contentment begins with trust. You cannot be content if you do not trust that God knows what you need. Trust is the soil in which contentment grows. It is the quiet assurance that the One who clothed the lilies and fed the sparrows has not forgotten you. When you live in trust, you release control, and in releasing control, you find freedom.

Freedom from anxiety, freedom from competition, freedom from the endless race to prove yourself. The truly content person no longer measures success by the applause of others, but by the approval of God. They no longer wake in fear of what might come, for they have anchored their joy in the unchanging character of their Creator.

Divine Wealth

Contentment does not ignore ambition, it purifies it. It allows you to dream without desperation, to pursue without pressure, to build without burden. It teaches you that growth is not the enemy of peace, and expansion is not the betrayal of rest. The one who has entered the covenant of contentment knows how to pursue excellence without losing stillness.

God delights in blessing His children, yet His greatest blessing is not always the abundance of things, but the abundance of peace. You can possess everything and still live empty, or possess little and overflow with joy. The difference lies not in possessions, but in perspective. Contentment transforms what you have into enough and what you dream into possible.

When you learn to be content, your spirit becomes unshakable. You are no longer thrown by the highs and lows of life. Promotion no longer inflates your pride, and delay no longer destroys your peace. You begin to understand that every season has its purpose, and every moment carries a message.

The Apostle Paul once wrote that he had learned the secret of being content in all circumstances, whether well-fed or hungry, living in plenty or in want. That secret was not resignation; it was revelation. He had discovered that strength does not come from circumstance, it comes from Christ. When your joy is rooted in Him, no loss can uproot it.

To live in divine contentment is to walk in divine rhythm. It is to move with the seasons of God without resisting or rushing them. It is to say, "If God has me here, then here is where I will grow." The content soul blooms in every environment, because it understands that every environment is an assignment.

Contentment is also a spiritual discipline. It must be cultivated through gratitude, protected through perspective, and strengthened through prayer. Gratitude opens your eyes to what is already beautiful

Divine Wealth

in your life. Perspective helps you see purpose even in the waiting. Prayer keeps you aligned with the Source of peace.

When you practice gratitude daily, you begin to see miracles in ordinary places. The sunrise becomes a sermon, the laughter of loved ones becomes a melody, the provision that once seemed small becomes proof of God's faithfulness. Gratitude enlarges your capacity to receive, not because it changes your circumstance, but because it changes your vision.

Gratitude is the gateway to joy. Joy is not found when everything is perfect, but when your heart is thankful even when things are not. Joy flows when you recognise that God's hand is present in the process, shaping you, refining you, preparing you for greater purpose. The covenant of contentment teaches you to live with open hands. To receive without greed, to give without fear, and to trust without hesitation. Open hands represent surrender, and surrender is the birthplace of peace. When you stop gripping the need to control outcomes, you make room for divine order to unfold.

Many believers spend their lives praying for more, but few pause to thank God for what already is. The danger of ungrateful desire is that it blinds you to blessings that are already in motion. What you call "not enough" may be the exact thing God is using to prepare you for more.

When you learn to appreciate small beginnings, heaven trusts you with larger ones. When you can celebrate someone else's success without envy, heaven knows you are ready for your own. The content heart does not compete; it completes. It understands that the same God who provides for one, provides for all.

Contentment does not mean stagnation; it means strength. It does not mean you stop dreaming, it means you stop doubting. The content believer can work diligently without being driven by fear. They can plan for the future without worrying about it, because their hope is anchored in eternity.

Divine Wealth

There is no peace like the peace of knowing you are where God wants you to be. That peace becomes your compass, your courage, and your comfort. It silences the noise of insecurity and reminds you that divine timing is never delayed.

When you live in the covenant of contentment, you become unbothered by the changing tides of the world. Markets may shift, economies may shake, but your provision flows from a higher source. You are not sustained by salary, but by the sovereignty of God.

Contentment is the antidote to fear. Fear says, "I will never have enough." Faith says, "God is more than enough." Every time you choose peace over panic, you strengthen your faith muscle. Every time you refuse to complain, you enlarge your gratitude. Every time you rest in God's promise, you participate in His provision.

The heart of contentment is intimacy. You cannot know peace apart from knowing the Prince of Peace. The deeper your relationship with Him, the less you crave validation from things. His presence becomes your greatest treasure. His word becomes your wealth. His love becomes your legacy.

The covenant of contentment is not about lowering expectation; it is about elevating trust. It is not about settling for less; it is about believing that what God provides is always enough for the purpose He has designed.

You learn that enough is not a number, it is a knowing. It is the divine confidence that you are fully provided for in this moment, fully equipped for this assignment, fully loved in this season. Enough is not the absence of lack, it is the awareness of grace.

As you mature in faith, you begin to see that peace is not the pause before progress, it is the presence of God in the process. When peace becomes your foundation, prosperity becomes your servant. You stop chasing what was never meant to fulfill you and start cherishing what was always meant to sustain you.

Divine Wealth

Every believer must come to the revelation that true abundance is not measured in possession, but in presence. To live in constant communion with God is to live in constant provision. His grace fills every gap, His strength meets every weakness, His timing perfects every detail.

The covenant of contentment protects the believer from the bondage of materialism. It keeps your heart free from the tyranny of comparison. The moment you stop comparing your journey to another's, you begin to see the masterpiece unfolding in your own. Comparison is the thief of joy, but gratitude is its guardian.

The content believer walks lightly, unburdened by the need to prove, impress, or outperform. Their peace becomes power. Their stillness becomes strength. They are rich in rest, abundant in joy, overflowing in purpose.

Contentment is not the absence of ambition, it is the sanctification of it. It does not tell you to stop dreaming, it teaches you to dream differently. When your ambition is purified by gratitude, it becomes aligned with heaven. You stop chasing for validation and start creating for impact. The restless pursuit of more gives way to a peaceful pursuit of purpose.

Every season of life carries its own rhythm, its own lessons, its own beauty. The content heart learns to dance in each one. When it rains, it drinks deeply. When the sun shines, it gives thanks. When the soil feels dry, it remembers that seeds grow in silence. The content soul knows that waiting is not wasting, it is preparation.

In a world obsessed with hurry, the Spirit still whispers, "Be still and know that I am God." Stillness is not inactivity, it is intentional awareness. It is the quiet strength that keeps you centered when everything else shifts. The truly prosperous person is not the one who owns the most, but the one who needs the least to feel whole. Contentment refines your desires. It exposes what is essential and what is empty. It teaches you to differentiate between what feeds the

Divine Wealth

ego and what fuels the spirit. The longer you walk with God, the more you realise that the deepest joys are often the simplest ones. Peace at home, love among family, laughter shared, health, friendship, and the presence of God , these are the treasures that cannot be purchased or replaced.

When your heart is content, even small blessings feel grand. A meal shared becomes sacred. A conversation becomes holy ground. The rhythm of everyday life becomes worship. Contentment baptises ordinary moments with eternal meaning.

But contentment is not automatic. It must be chosen daily. The flesh resists simplicity; it craves applause. It wants to be seen, heard, admired, validated. Yet the Spirit reminds you that true security is not found in recognition, but in relationship. When you anchor your identity in God's approval, the opinions of others lose their power to shake you.

You will know you have entered the covenant of contentment when peace begins to follow you. You no longer force outcomes. You no longer feel the need to prove your worth through constant action. You no longer panic when doors close, because you trust that divine redirection is better than human ambition. You begin to walk slower, speak softer, love deeper.

The content believer understands that God's pace is perfect. Every delay has design. Every silence has strategy. Every detour has direction. To live in this awareness is to live in rest, even while working, to move with grace even while growing.

Contentment is also the posture of strength in uncertainty. When the future feels unclear, contentment says, "I trust the One who holds it." It replaces anxiety with assurance. It transforms waiting into worship. The content soul can rest even in transition because it knows that God's hand is steady even when the path is not.

Many people fear contentment because they confuse it with complacency. But the two are not the same. Complacency settles

Divine Wealth

because of fear. Contentment rests because of faith. Complacency stops growing. Contentment grows in peace. The content believer remains teachable, adaptable, and ready, not driven by worry but by wisdom.

When you cultivate contentment, you begin to carry a quiet authority. You are no longer moved by every change in circumstance. Your peace becomes contagious. People drawn to noise will begin to seek your stillness. Your calm presence will become a sermon without words, a reflection of the Kingdom within you.

Contentment is the foundation of emotional intelligence. It allows you to respond rather than react. It gives you time to breathe before you speak, to listen before you judge, to pray before you decide. The world rushes, but those at peace with God never hurry, for they know the Shepherd always leads on time.

As you grow in this grace, you will begin to notice that contentment fuels creativity. When your mind is not clouded by comparison, your ideas flow more freely. When you are not burdened by fear, your spirit becomes more inventive. Peace makes room for purpose to speak.

The covenant of contentment also transforms your relationship with money. You no longer see it as the source of peace, but as the servant of it. You manage it wisely, but you do not worship it. You use it to create freedom for yourself and others, but it never defines your worth. In your hands, money becomes ministry, a means to bless, build, and give back.

Financial contentment does not mean financial passivity. It means understanding that prosperity is a journey of stewardship, not stress. You plan, save, and invest, but you do so with calm, not compulsion. You sow, but you do not strive. You work, but you do not worship work. You trust that increase comes not from anxiety, but from alignment.

Divine Wealth

When you live this way, you become unshakeable. Economic storms may come, but your peace remains intact because your economy is divine. The same God who provided manna in the wilderness can provide wisdom in modern times. He can open new streams, create new partnerships, inspire new ideas, and multiply what you have.

The covenant of contentment protects your focus. It keeps you from being distracted by trends and comparisons. You do not waste energy chasing every opportunity, for you know not every opportunity is ordained. You learn to say no with confidence because you are no longer led by fear of missing out, but by faith in divine timing.

There is power in saying no. Every no rooted in peace becomes an invitation to something better. When you decline what is not aligned, you make space for what is meant. The content heart has learned to distinguish between open doors and divine doors.

As contentment matures, it becomes compassion. You begin to see the needs of others with softer eyes. Because you no longer live in scarcity, you can give freely. You do not give from guilt, but from grace. Your giving becomes natural, joyful, and generous.

The content soul gives without hesitation because it knows it can never outgive God. Every act of generosity becomes an echo of trust. Giving becomes an extension of peace, a visible sign that you believe in divine sufficiency.

Contentment and generosity are twins in the spirit. One cannot thrive without the other. Contentment gives birth to generosity, and generosity sustains contentment. When you give, you remind yourself that there is more where that came from. You declare that heaven's supply is endless, and that you are only a steward of its flow.

The covenant of contentment turns every transaction into transformation. What once was ordinary spending becomes spiritual sowing. What once was obligation becomes opportunity. The content believer lives with an awareness that every action can reflect heaven's heart.

Divine Wealth

True joy comes not from acquiring, but from aligning. When your life aligns with God's rhythm, even your smallest actions carry eternal significance. The way you speak, spend, share, and serve all become reflections of divine order.

Contentment is not something you achieve once; it is something you maintain daily. You feed it with prayer, nurture it with gratitude, and protect it with boundaries. The enemy cannot steal your joy if your contentment is guarded by prayer.

Each day, choose peace. Each morning, speak gratitude. Each evening, rest in trust. Let your routine become a rhythm of contentment. Over time, that rhythm becomes your reality.

As you live in this covenant, you will begin to see how peace multiplies blessings. The calmer you are, the clearer you hear God's direction. The more thankful you are, the more reasons you find to give thanks. The more generous you are, the more grace flows back to you. Peace does not pause prosperity, it multiplies it.

This is the paradox of the Kingdom: those who stop chasing begin to attract. Those who stop grasping begin to grow. Those who rest in God's timing begin to rise in His favour. The covenant of contentment is not a lesser life, it is a higher one. It is the life where prosperity and peace are no longer separate, but the same.

When you reach that place, every breath feels like worship, every act feels like service, every day feels like grace renewed. You live not in anxiety about tomorrow, but in awe of today. You do not fear what comes next, because you know who holds it.

And in that peace, you find freedom. Freedom from fear, from comparison, from striving, from scarcity. Freedom to live with open hands and a full heart. Freedom to enjoy what you have without guilt and to pursue what's next without greed.

That is the covenant of contentment. It is the still water where your soul finds rest, the fertile ground where your faith grows stronger,

Divine Wealth

and the sacred space where heaven and earth meet in the quiet assurance that, truly, God is enough.

Divine Wealth

Chapter 12: The Power of Kingdom Partnership, How Collective Faith Creates Unstoppable Impact

Divine Wealth

When God designed the Kingdom, He never intended for His children to walk alone. From the very beginning, His vision was community, His language was unity, and His plan was partnership. Every divine movement in history was born not through isolation, but through collaboration. Heaven moves when hearts align.

The true measure of Kingdom wealth is not how much one person accumulates, but how much a community can build together. The power of Kingdom partnership is the miracle of multiplied faith. One person can plant, another can water, but it is God who gives the increase. When believers unite in purpose, their individual strength becomes exponential.

Partnership in the Kingdom is more than cooperation; it is covenant. It is two or more people agreeing in faith, bound by shared vision and divine purpose. When this kind of unity is established, heaven responds. For where two or three are gathered in His name, there He is in the midst of them.

God blesses unity because unity mirrors His own nature. The Father, the Son, and the Holy Spirit exist in perfect harmony, working as one. This divine blueprint shows that power is multiplied in togetherness. Isolation weakens purpose, but connection strengthens destiny.

When you walk in divine partnership, your gifts find their rightful place. No single person carries the fullness of what the world needs. Each believer is a fragment of God's greater picture. Partnership is the puzzle that allows every piece to reveal the masterpiece.

In the Kingdom, collaboration is not competition. It is complement. Each person brings what the other lacks. One may carry the vision, another the strategy, another the resource, and another the faith to activate it. When combined under the same Spirit, these differences no longer divide; they define the design of God's purpose.

Partnership in the Kingdom requires humility. It means recognising that you are not the entire story, but a chapter in God's larger

Divine Wealth

narrative. It means being willing to stand beside others, not above them. The proud build empires; the humble build eternity.
When believers walk in harmony, they create a current of spiritual power that no opposition can withstand. The enemy fears unity more than wealth, because wealth without unity divides, but unity without wealth still multiplies influence. When the people of God move as one, they become unstoppable.
True Kingdom partnership is rooted in love. Love that serves rather than controls, that uplifts rather than competes, that gives rather than withholds. Love that sees another's success as part of its own. Love that understands that in the Kingdom, your win is my win, and my victory strengthens yours.
The early church in Acts was a living portrait of divine partnership. They shared everything they had, breaking bread with gladness and simplicity of heart. They lived in one accord, and the result was revival. Unity opened the floodgates of heaven. Souls were added daily, miracles multiplied, and the Spirit flowed freely.
This same principle remains alive today. When people come together with pure hearts and common faith, the supernatural becomes natural. Collective obedience creates a climate for collective miracles. When one sows, and another waters, and all give glory to God, increase becomes inevitable.
Partnership is sacred because it carries accountability. Alone, you can move fast, but together, you move far. Partnership keeps you steady, balanced, and aligned. It refines your vision through shared wisdom and strengthens your resolve through shared faith.
God never intended for wealth to remain in the hands of one. He designed prosperity to flow through networks of faith, through families, through churches, through communities. Every resource He provides is meant to multiply through relationship.
Divine partnership also protects you from the illusion of self-sufficiency. When you walk with others, you are constantly reminded

Divine Wealth

that every success is a shared grace. You begin to see that progress is not just the fruit of your labour, but the outcome of collective faithfulness.

Partnership transforms prosperity from personal achievement into communal advancement. It turns individual blessings into Kingdom building. It breaks the cycle of selfish ambition and replaces it with shared vision.

The greatest Kingdom projects in history were not achieved by one person, but by united hearts. Noah built the ark with his family, Moses led a nation with Aaron, Joshua conquered with Caleb, David ruled with mighty men, Nehemiah rebuilt Jerusalem with workers shoulder to shoulder, Jesus walked with twelve. Every divine assignment grows through divine connection.

When you find your divine partners, destiny accelerates. The right people do not just support you; they stretch you. They see your potential when you forget it, they pray when you are weary, they hold faith when your hands tremble. The anointing flows stronger when shared.

Partnership also demands discernment. Not every alliance is divine. The wrong partnerships drain energy, dilute vision, and distract purpose. True Kingdom partnership must be birthed in prayer, tested through purpose, and sealed by peace. The right connection will always bring clarity, not confusion.

To partner God's way, you must walk in transparency and trust. Hidden motives break unity. Selfish ambition poisons collaboration. But when you walk in truth, humility, and shared faith, partnership becomes a mirror of heaven's harmony.

When believers gather with one heart and one goal , to glorify God and advance His Kingdom , supernatural synergy takes over. The impossible becomes inevitable. Ideas turn into movements. Vision turns into impact. What one could never do alone becomes effortless together.

Divine Wealth

God designed partnership to multiply not only influence, but joy. There is joy in shared labour, joy in shared victory, joy in knowing that you are part of something eternal. When you build with others in love, your joy is complete, for you are fulfilling the command to love one another as Christ loved you.

Kingdom partnership is not just for building ministries; it is for building nations, economies, and communities. It is the divine structure that turns spiritual conviction into tangible change. When believers collaborate with excellence, they show the world what heaven's order looks like on earth.

Each person carries a piece of divine capacity. Some are dreamers, others are builders, others are sustainers. The dreamer imagines, the builder executes, the sustainer preserves. Together, they reflect the rhythm of creation itself , vision, formation, continuation. This is how heaven works.

The power of Kingdom partnership is that it outlives you. When you build alone, your work ends with your lifetime. When you build together, your impact becomes generational. Partnership ensures that what God started through you will continue long after you are gone. Partnership is the economy of the Kingdom. It is the way God circulates blessing. When you pour into others, others pour into you. When you give freely, the flow never stops. When communities give together, they attract the supernatural.

You will know that a partnership is divine when it multiplies peace, purpose, and presence. God's hand rests where His people dwell in unity. Every divine partnership carries divine protection. When hearts beat as one, heaven guards their work.

Kingdom partnership requires maturity. It calls for the ability to celebrate another's success without envy, to lead without pride, to follow without fear, and to forgive without condition. It is not built on convenience, but on covenant. It is not sustained by emotion, but by devotion.

Divine Wealth

When you build in partnership, you realise that the goal is not personal recognition, but collective redemption. It is not about your name being remembered, but His name being revealed. True Kingdom builders care more about legacy than credit, more about impact than applause.

The world glorifies independence, but heaven glorifies interdependence. Independence says, "I don't need anyone." Interdependence says, "Together, we reflect God's fullness." Every relationship in the Kingdom is designed to reveal a facet of His character. When we work together, we reveal Him more completely.

Partnership is a ministry of trust. It means believing that God can speak through someone else. It means valuing another person's anointing as much as your own. It means understanding that the oil flows through connection, not competition.

When you walk with others in unity, you create a divine echo that reaches heaven. Agreement amplifies authority. A united prayer shakes strongholds that single voices could never move. A united effort transforms cities that individual effort could never reach.

Kingdom partnership is the heartbeat of revival. Revival does not come through one voice, but through many voices crying out in harmony. It does not come through one leader, but through surrendered hearts moving as one. When the church becomes one body in purpose, heaven releases power without measure.

The covenant of partnership teaches that you are not meant to do everything, but you are meant to do your part. The beauty of the body is in its diversity. The hand cannot do what the heart does, nor the eye what the foot does. Each part is vital, each role sacred.

When you understand this, jealousy disappears. You stop comparing your lane to another's, because you realise that the road to destiny is wide enough for all who walk in faith. The strength of the Kingdom is not uniformity, but unity.

Divine Wealth

Partnership is not a project; it is a process. It is the constant choosing of unity over pride, forgiveness over resentment, purpose over preference. Every divine relationship requires maintenance. The same way you nurture your relationship with God through prayer and intimacy, you must nurture your partnerships through patience and understanding.

Godly relationships are gardens. They must be watered with encouragement, pruned with honesty, and guarded with prayer. Neglect causes weeds to grow, but care causes fruit to flourish. When you invest in your partnerships with intention, you create an ecosystem of grace where every seed of faith can bloom.

True partnership requires vulnerability. You cannot connect deeply without allowing others to see who you truly are. Transparency is not weakness; it is trust. The greatest strength in unity comes from authenticity. Pretence builds walls, but honesty builds bridges.

When you are surrounded by people who love God and love you enough to tell you the truth, you are safe. Correction from a friend is better than flattery from a crowd. The right partnerships sharpen your discernment, challenge your character, and keep you accountable to your calling.

Partnerships built on prayer endure what pressure cannot break. When believers pray together, they synchronise their spirits. Prayer unites intentions, aligns motives, and keeps hearts soft. When prayer becomes the language of partnership, offence loses its power and love grows deeper.

To build partnerships that last, you must lead with humility. Humility does not mean thinking less of yourself; it means thinking of yourself less. It means being willing to listen, to learn, and to yield. The humble heart attracts divine favour because it reflects the heart of Christ.

The most powerful partnerships are not those where everyone agrees on everything, but those where everyone honours one another

Divine Wealth

despite differences. Unity is not the absence of disagreement; it is the presence of love that transcends it. When you prioritise relationship over being right, heaven smiles upon your work.

God uses partnerships to refine His people. Working with others exposes both your strengths and your weaknesses. It reveals your capacity for patience, your ability to forgive, and your willingness to grow. Every partnership is a mirror that helps you see yourself through the eyes of grace.

Partnership also teaches endurance. Not every season will feel easy, not every plan will unfold smoothly, but those who persist in faith together will see the fruit of perseverance. What takes one a lifetime can take a community a moment when God blesses their collective effort.

You must learn to celebrate progress, not just perfection. Every small victory shared with others is a seed of encouragement that strengthens the next step. The joy of building together is not only in the finished work, but in the shared journey.

When God looks upon His people, He does not measure their success by size, but by unity. He does not ask how big your project became, but how pure your partnership remained. Heaven rewards harmony because harmony reveals holiness.

Kingdom partnerships multiply not only results, but revelation. When people of faith gather to work, ideas emerge that would never surface in isolation. One person sees a problem, another sees a solution, another sees the system that makes it sustainable. Together, they build what none could conceive alone.

Partnerships also unlock provision. Many believers pray for resources without realising that the resource is often hidden in a relationship. God hides His blessings inside people. When you honour the right connections, you access divine supply.

A single tree cannot create a forest, but a forest can change the climate. A single flame may light a room, but a network of torches

Divine Wealth

can light a city. The Church, when united, becomes that forest of faith, that city on a hill whose light cannot be hidden.

When believers collaborate, they bring heaven's solutions into earth's problems. Poverty, injustice, division, and despair cannot withstand a unified people filled with the Spirit of God. Partnership is heaven's answer to earth's brokenness.

God uses collective faith to change systems, not just hearts. One voice can preach truth, but many voices together can transform nations. The Church was never meant to exist as scattered sparks, but as a wildfire of love and truth burning across the world.

True partnership is generational. It does not end with one age group or one leader; it flows forward, empowering those who come next. When you build with others, you create a foundation upon which future generations can stand taller. The greatest legacy is not what you leave behind, but who you raise to continue.

Kingdom partnership requires vision beyond self. It means thinking generationally, planting trees under whose shade you may never sit. It means giving time, wisdom, and resources so that others can go further than you ever could.

The more you give to others, the more you expand your eternal influence. Heaven keeps perfect record of every investment made into another life. The rewards of unity are not only temporal, but eternal. The relationships you nurture here are echoes of the communion you will share in heaven.

To build Kingdom partnerships that endure, you must also master forgiveness. Offence is the quickest destroyer of divine connection. The enemy cannot destroy a powerful community, so he tries to divide it. He plants seeds of misunderstanding, jealousy, and pride. Forgiveness uproots them before they take root.

You do not forgive because the other person deserves it; you forgive because you deserve peace. Forgiveness restores flow. It breaks chains that block collaboration. It reopens the channels through

Divine Wealth

which grace can travel. When you forgive, you disarm the enemy and invite God back into the relationship.

True partnership cannot exist without grace. Grace covers imperfection, allowing love to prevail. Grace allows you to see others through the lens of compassion instead of criticism. Grace transforms teams into families, and families into movements.

When grace governs your partnerships, you begin to experience the power of collective anointing. There is a spiritual strength that only manifests in shared purpose. The oil that flowed from Aaron's head ran down his beard and onto his garments. It did not stay at the top; it spread across the whole body. The same anointing that covers one in unity covers all.

Partnerships must also be prophetic. This means they look forward, not backward. They are guided by vision, not nostalgia. They build toward what is coming, not what has been. Prophetic partnership speaks life into tomorrow and invests hope into generations yet unborn.

You build prophetic partnerships when you dream together, pray together, plan together, and act together. Every meeting becomes ministry, every conversation becomes collaboration, every agreement becomes alignment.

To sustain these partnerships, integrity must be your anchor. Without integrity, even the most gifted group will crumble. Trust is the currency of heaven's economy. Once broken, it takes time to rebuild, but when preserved, it compounds into influence.

When you build with integrity, you create a testimony that speaks louder than words. People will trust what they see more than what they hear. When your unity remains pure through pressure, the world takes notice. The world is not changed by sermons alone, but by the witness of unity lived out in love.

Every believer has a role in this great symphony of partnership. Some will lead, some will serve, some will give, some will pray. None is

Divine Wealth

lesser, all are needed. The harmony of the body depends on the contribution of every part.

If you are called to lead, lead with humility. If you are called to serve, serve with joy. If you are called to give, give with gladness. Each act of obedience strengthens the collective sound of heaven on earth.

The greatest partnerships are those that keep Christ at the centre. When Jesus is the focus, unity endures. When ego becomes the focus, division begins. Keep the cross at the core of every collaboration. Let love be the language and grace be the goal.

When believers unite across nations, denominations, and backgrounds, heaven rejoices. The Kingdom is not defined by borders or labels, but by love. Unity is not uniformity; it is harmony among difference. When diversity works together in love, it reflects the creative brilliance of the Creator Himself.

God is raising communities of Kingdom builders in this generation. Men and women who will not compete for spotlight, but share the flame. They will build schools, hospitals, businesses, and ministries that transform societies from the inside out. They will understand that wealth, influence, and wisdom are not for self-glory, but for shared growth.

The future belongs to those who can partner with purpose. The era of isolated ambition is ending, and the age of divine collaboration is rising. The next great move of God will not come through one voice, but through many voices harmonising in faith.

When Kingdom partnership reaches its fullness, the earth will see what heaven has always intended , a family united under one Father, a people working together for one purpose, and a generation that gives glory to one Name.

This is the power of partnership. It is not just what you build, but how you build it. It is not just who stands beside you, but Who stands within you. When hearts beat in rhythm with heaven, and

Divine Wealth

hands work in harmony on earth, miracles become the normal language of life.

Together, we are unstoppable. Together, we are unbreakable.

Together, we are the living testimony that heaven's greatest works are written not in isolation, but in unity. And when we build together, we build forever.

Divine Wealth

Chapter 13: Legacy and Light, Becoming the Bridge for Future Generations

Divine Wealth

Every generation is a continuation of the last, a living testimony of what was sown before. None of us begins where we began; we all begin where someone else left off. The hands that raised you, the words that shaped you, the sacrifices that protected you , they built the ground upon which you now stand. Legacy is not an event; it is a river, flowing quietly through time, carrying the essence of every faithful heart that poured into it.

Legacy is the whisper of eternity in human form. It is the echo of obedience that outlives its moment. It is the reflection of divine purpose through the lives we touch, the truths we pass on, and the light we kindle in others. Every good work, every act of love, every seed of wisdom becomes part of this sacred inheritance that does not fade with time, but deepens with it.

You were never meant to live as an isolated chapter; you were meant to write continuation. God does not bless you so that His story ends with you; He blesses you so that His story continues through you. When He increases you, He is entrusting you with a responsibility , to build something that outlasts comfort, to invest in what cannot perish, to leave the world brighter than you found it.

The true wealth of a believer is not measured by accumulation, but by continuation. It is not what you store, but what you sow. It is not what you keep, but what you cultivate. Legacy is not ownership; it is stewardship extended through time. It is the understanding that your life is a bridge between what was and what will be.

Every generation carries a torch, and the question is never whether the flame will burn, but whether it will be passed on. Legacy is light that travels from hand to hand, from heart to heart. The moment you stop thinking only of your own survival and begin to think of the impact your life will have on those who follow, you have stepped into divine maturity.

God designed legacy as the rhythm of His Kingdom. The promises He made to Abraham flowed through Isaac and Jacob, down through

Divine Wealth

generations, shaping nations and fulfilling prophecy. God's blessing is never single-seasoned; it is generational. His intention is always continuity. What begins in faith must continue in faith.

To build legacy, you must see beyond the present. Vision is the blueprint of inheritance. Those who build legacy are those who see the invisible and prepare for it. They understand that every choice is a seed, every decision a direction, every habit a heritage. What you model in your daily life becomes a silent sermon to those who will come after you.

Children do not learn from advice; they learn from example. The next generation will not be moved by what we say about faith, but by how we live it. They will not inherit our words unless they can see them reflected in our walk. Legacy is lived truth. It is faith in motion. When you begin to live for legacy, you stop living for applause and start living for alignment. You are no longer satisfied with temporary victories; you seek eternal ones. You no longer measure success by what you possess, but by who you prepare. You realise that your greatest accomplishment may not be something you do, but someone you raise, inspire, or empower.

Legacy begins in private long before it manifests in public. It is formed in prayer, shaped in sacrifice, and confirmed in consistency. The unseen choices of integrity, the quiet moments of surrender, the faithfulness when no one applauds , these are the foundations upon which divine legacies are built.

God is not looking for people who will be impressive for a moment; He is seeking those who will be impactful for generations. The legacy you leave is determined by the values you live. If you walk in faith, you plant faith. If you lead with love, you leave love. If you serve with humility, humility becomes your heritage.

You cannot pass on what you do not possess. To leave a legacy of faith, you must first live a life of faith. To leave a legacy of wisdom, you must first walk in understanding. To leave a legacy of abundance,

Divine Wealth

you must first learn stewardship. Every seed you plant in obedience becomes a tree under which someone else will find rest.
Legacy is both inheritance and invitation. It is inheritance because it flows from those who came before, and invitation because it calls those who come next to go further. You are the recipient of someone else's faith, and the steward of someone else's future. You stand between what was and what will be, called to honour the past by preparing the future.
The legacy of light begins when you understand that wealth without wisdom fades, but wisdom with worship endures. True wealth multiplies when it is shared, not hoarded. The purpose of prosperity is not to make your name great, but to keep God's work alive through your life. Every resource you have is a seed of legacy waiting for purpose.
You build legacy when you turn success into service. Every open door becomes an opportunity to lift others higher. Every blessing becomes a bridge. The moment you decide that what you have will serve others, your influence multiplies. The more you pour out, the more heaven pours in.
Legacy is not limited to family or bloodline; it extends through faithline. Those who share your faith become part of your spiritual lineage. The people you mentor, encourage, and inspire are your children in destiny. The souls you help awaken are your eternal heirs. Legacy transcends genetics; it is the heritage of spirit.
Building legacy requires intention. It will not happen by accident. You must decide daily that what you are doing today is not only for you, but for those who will come after. You must think generationally, act sacrificially, and live purposefully. Every time you choose obedience over ease, you are protecting a future you may never see.
You will know you are walking in legacy when your dreams begin to include names you will never meet. When your prayers begin to

Divine Wealth

mention generations not yet born. When you build systems, institutions, or ideas that will serve others long after you are gone. That is when you begin to partner with eternity.

There is a difference between a moment of greatness and a lifetime of impact. Greatness draws attention, but legacy builds transformation. One may make headlines, but the other makes history. The greatest men and women of God were not those who shone the brightest for a day, but those who built lamps that others could carry long after.

Every act of obedience sends ripples into time. You may never know the full impact of what you do in faith, but heaven does. The prayer you pray today may protect your descendants a century from now. The generosity you show may ignite a movement of giving in hearts yet unborn. Legacy is not only what you see; it is what heaven sustains through your faithfulness.

Legacy is built when your story becomes someone else's starting point. Every breakthrough you achieve becomes the baseline for another's belief. Every mountain you move clears a path for another to climb higher. You become a living bridge, carrying others across the waters of uncertainty toward their own promised land.

Legacy is the holy echo of your existence. It is your yes to God reverberating through time. It is the sound of obedience amplified across generations. It is proof that faith never dies; it multiplies.

But legacy requires surrender. You cannot cling to everything and still create something that lasts. To build what endures, you must be willing to release what is temporary. You must live with open hands, ready to let go when God says, "Now give it away."

Your legacy is not the wealth you keep, but the wealth you release. It is not the name you preserve, but the name you lift higher. It is not the comfort you protect, but the calling you pursue. The more you give, the more you guarantee that your light will continue to shine beyond your lifetime.

Divine Wealth

There is a divine principle that every seed must die before it multiplies. The same is true of legacy. It is born when you stop living only for yourself. It is born when you understand that your highest purpose is not self-preservation, but self-giving. Legacy is resurrection written through generosity.

When you begin to think of what will remain after you are gone, wisdom takes root in your decisions. You begin to value principles over pleasure, purpose over popularity, legacy over luxury. You start investing not only in what you can see, but in what will last. You start speaking words that will outlive your voice.

Legacy is not a destination; it is a lifestyle. It is how you show up, how you lead, how you forgive, how you give, how you love. It is every act of faith multiplied across time. The light you carry is not meant to be hidden; it is meant to be handed over.

To live for legacy is to understand that your greatest work may never bear your name. It may bloom in another's hands. It may flourish in another's field. Yet it will still carry your fragrance, because you planted it with love.

The most powerful legacies are invisible. They are not built of wealth alone, but of spirit, conviction, compassion, and courage. They cannot be destroyed by markets or governments. They live on in the hearts they have healed and the lives they have changed.

You were never meant to fade quietly into time; you were meant to shine as part of a divine continuum. Every believer is both a recipient and a transmitter of glory. What began with the faith of our ancestors continues through our obedience. And one day, someone will stand upon the foundation you laid and build higher still.

Legacy is not the end of your story; it is the continuation of God's. You are the vessel through which eternity writes its next chapter. Every act of love, every moment of integrity, every offering of generosity is a sentence in that sacred script. You are not only living history; you are writing heaven's record.

Divine Wealth

Legacy becomes real when you start preparing others to walk in what you once prayed for. It is one thing to build; it is another to teach someone how to build. The true measure of success is not how much you can hold, but how much you can hand over.

Every generation must be trained, not only through knowledge, but through example. You can give people wealth, but without wisdom, it will fade. You can give them opportunity, but without character, it will crumble. The most powerful inheritance you can pass on is not what you leave in their hands, but what you plant in their hearts.

The next generation does not need more instruction; they need more demonstration. They need to see what faith looks like in motion, what generosity feels like in action, what humility sounds like in speech. They are not waiting for perfection; they are waiting for authenticity. When they see your light, they will know how to ignite their own.

To raise heirs of faith, you must live with intentional transparency. Let them see your prayers, not just your victories. Let them hear your gratitude, not just your goals. Let them witness how you walk through difficulty, how you rise from failure, how you return to joy. The next generation learns not from a life without storms, but from a life that continues to praise God through them.

God's design for generational continuity is mentorship. Every Paul needs a Timothy. Every Naomi a Ruth. Every Elijah an Elisha. Legacy is sustained through relationship. You must pour into someone as others poured into you. Knowledge that is not shared becomes dormant; wisdom that is not taught becomes lost.

When you pour into others, you multiply your influence beyond time. The seeds of your wisdom take root in lives that will grow long after you have gone. The prayers you prayed for them will hover over their journeys, guiding them in unseen ways. What you pour in private will echo in their public purpose.

Divine Wealth

Legacy is not about control; it is about cultivation. You are not called to create replicas of yourself, but reflections of Christ. The goal of spiritual inheritance is not to reproduce your image, but to reproduce His. When you mentor others, you are teaching them to listen to God's voice, not just yours.

To create generational wealth in God's design, you must first redefine what wealth means. It is not limited to finances or possessions. True wealth is the ability to produce good fruit. It is the capacity to generate blessing from within, to turn ideas into impact, to transform revelation into restoration.

Generational wealth begins with spiritual foundations. It is faith before fortune, principle before profit, obedience before opportunity. When these roots are deep, the fruit will endure. A family that is rich in faith can never truly be poor, for they hold the currency of heaven. Financial inheritance without spiritual discipline is fragile. Wealth passed down without vision becomes burden instead of blessing. But when faith and wisdom accompany provision, every generation begins higher than the one before. This is the divine pattern of increase.

You are called to break cycles that confined your ancestors and establish new ones for those who will come after you. You are called to turn lack into legacy, fear into faith, survival into significance. Every chain you break becomes freedom for someone else. Every prayer you pray becomes protection for those who will carry your name.

Legacy requires structure. Vision must be followed by systems. Passion must be joined with preparation. Faith builds the foundation, but diligence constructs the walls. You must plan not only for what God has done, but for what He will do through those who follow.

A wise builder leaves clear blueprints. The wisdom you document today becomes instruction for tomorrow. Write down what God teaches you. Record what He reveals. Speak openly of your journey.

Divine Wealth

Share your testimony freely, for your story carries keys that unlock others.

When you live for legacy, you become less concerned with timelines and more focused on timelines eternal. You realise that your season is not the whole story, but part of a divine sequence. You may begin something that another will finish. You may water seeds that another will harvest. You may prepare ground for fruit you will never taste, yet your reward will be the joy of knowing it will feed others.

Legacy demands perseverance. The work of building for the future is rarely glamorous. It is consistent, humble, patient. It requires you to keep sowing when results are unseen, to keep building when applause is absent, to keep believing when others doubt. But heaven measures not how fast you finish, but how faithfully you follow through.

You must also protect your legacy. The enemy cannot destroy what God has blessed, but he can distract what God has built. Distraction is one of the greatest threats to divine inheritance. Stay focused on your assignment. Do not dilute your anointing by chasing recognition. Do not waste energy fighting battles that do not belong to your purpose. Guard the work that God has entrusted to you.

You protect legacy through prayer. Prayer is the wall around inheritance. It seals what God has given and shields it from what the enemy attempts. When you pray over your family, your work, your disciples, your community, you are building spiritual fortresses that will stand long after you are gone.

You must also trust that legacy will evolve. The next generation may not do things the way you did, but that does not mean they are wrong. God moves in seasons, and each generation carries a different grace for its time. Legacy is not control; it is continuity. Your role is to provide roots strong enough for branches to reach higher.

A true legacy outlives trends and transcends time. It adapts without losing its essence, evolves without losing its foundation. The Spirit

Divine Wealth

that began a work in you will continue it through them. The melody may change, but the message remains.

To sustain legacy, you must keep your heart pure. Motive determines momentum. If you build for God's glory, your work will remain. If you build for self, it will fade. The difference between empire and Kingdom is intention. One seeks power; the other seeks purpose. Legacy flourishes when humility reigns. The moment you believe your success belongs to you, it begins to wither. But when you continually give God the glory, He keeps watering the seeds you planted. Humility keeps your legacy alive.

You will know you are walking in legacy when your prayers begin to sound like blessings over others. When you speak more of those who come next than of yourself. When your vision expands beyond your lifetime. When you start to live less for memory and more for meaning.

At the heart of legacy is love. Love that gives without counting, love that builds without boasting, love that serves without expectation. Love that refuses to end with one lifetime. Love that believes the best, even when unseen. This is the kind of love that leaves footprints in eternity.

When your time on earth comes to an end, what will remain is not the applause you received, but the lives you changed. Not the possessions you held, but the purpose you fulfilled. Not the comfort you enjoyed, but the courage you displayed. Legacy is heaven's measure of a life well lived.

To finish well is to finish with peace. It is to look back and know that you did not hoard your light, but shared it. It is to see that your journey became a map for others, that your faith became their fire, that your surrender became their strength.

God delights in those who finish their race with grace. The final chapter of your story is not about wealth or recognition, but about faithfulness. The question will not be how much you accumulated,

Divine Wealth

but how much you gave, how deeply you loved, how faithfully you believed.

You are called to be a bridge, not a barrier. A bridge connects what was to what will be. A bridge carries others to places they could not reach alone. A bridge is built to be walked on, but its strength remains unseen beneath the surface. The beauty of legacy is not in being noticed, but in being necessary.

Your life is a divine bridge between generations. Your obedience today opens doors for others tomorrow. Your generosity funds missions you may never see. Your prayers sustain people you will never meet. Your name may fade, but your faith will live on.

The light of legacy is eternal. It cannot be extinguished by time, nor confined by mortality. It shines through those you have touched, through the faith you have inspired, through the love you have given. It is the eternal spark of God's glory reflected in your obedience.

As you live in this awareness, your days take on new weight. You begin to see your time as sacred currency, your words as seeds, your relationships as ministries. You live not for recognition, but for resonance. Every step becomes stewardship. Every breath becomes worship.

And when you have done all that God has called you to do, you will rest knowing that your life was not lived in vain. You will rest knowing that your light still burns in those who carry your flame. You will rest knowing that you were faithful, fruitful, and free. Legacy is not the end of your story; it is the beginning of someone else's. You are the bridge, the builder, the bearer of light. What you have carried will continue. What you have planted will grow. What you have believed will manifest. This is the eternal beauty of legacy. It never ends; it simply transforms.

Divine Wealth

Chapter 14: The Divine Exchange, Where Faith Meets Fruitfulness

Divine Wealth

There comes a moment in every believer's journey when you realise that everything you have ever desired was never truly about possession, but about partnership. You begin to see that prosperity is not proof of your strength, but a reflection of God's generosity. You understand that all your striving, all your building, all your earning were never the goal; they were preparation for something greater, something eternal, something divine.

The true purpose of wealth is worship. Not in the sense of songs or ceremonies, but in the quiet posture of surrender that says, "God, everything I have belongs to You." It is in that moment that the divine exchange begins. You give Him what you thought was yours, and He gives you what could never be bought. You release your hold on resources, and He releases His rivers of grace. You stop chasing security, and you start walking in peace.

Fruitfulness is born where faith and surrender meet. It is not forced, it flows. It is not earned, it emerges. It is the natural result of a life aligned with divine purpose. When you live in that rhythm, your work becomes worship, your giving becomes gratitude, and your prosperity becomes praise. Every act of obedience becomes a seed of abundance, every act of service becomes a harvest of joy.

God never called you to a life of scarcity. He called you to a life of stewardship. You were not created to live from fear, but from faith. You were not designed to survive on crumbs, but to cultivate gardens. The same God who clothed the lilies and fed the sparrows has placed His Spirit in you to create, to multiply, to bless. The divine exchange is not only about giving up; it is about growing up, stepping into maturity where you recognise that God's provision is perfect and His purpose is limitless.

When you see yourself as a vessel, not an owner, everything changes. Money no longer holds you; it serves you. Success no longer defines you; it refines you. You stop counting your blessings and start

Divine Wealth

multiplying them. You realise that the point was never to gather more, but to give more, to serve more, to love more.

There is a holy rhythm to divine abundance. It begins with receiving, matures in releasing, and blossoms in replenishing. You receive from God what you need. You release it through generosity and service. And in doing so, you are replenished with new grace, new wisdom, new vision. The more you give, the more heaven trusts you with. This is the sacred law of Kingdom economics: generosity sustains increase.

Your wealth was never meant to end with you. You are the river, not the reservoir. A reservoir keeps, but a river carries. A reservoir fills, but a river flows. A reservoir grows stagnant, but a river stays alive. The more you let your blessings flow through you, the fresher they remain. The more you release, the more you receive.

Every good gift from God is meant to return to Him, multiplied in love. That is the divine exchange, the cycle of creation, redemption, and continuation. God gives you seed. You plant it in faith. It bears fruit for His Kingdom. And from that fruit, new seeds are born. Every time you give, you join that holy cycle. You become a co-creator with God, shaping the world through obedience.

This is what it means to be rich in God's way: to hold abundance lightly and purpose tightly. To walk in the confidence that your prosperity is not your identity, but your instrument. To see money not as a master, but as a messenger of grace. To live in such a way that your financial life becomes an altar where heaven and earth meet. God's ultimate desire is not for you to be rich, but for you to be righteous in how you use riches. When righteousness governs wealth, prosperity becomes purpose, and purpose becomes worship. When you live this way, you no longer fear lack, because you know the Source cannot run dry. You no longer chase approval, because you know your identity is secure in Christ. You no longer measure worth by numbers, but by impact.

Divine Wealth

Every believer is invited into this divine exchange. It is an invitation to trade anxiety for trust, greed for gratitude, scarcity for sufficiency, and striving for surrender. It is the moment you stop asking, "What can I gain?" and start asking, "What can I give?" It is when wealth transforms from what you chase into what you channel.

As you step into this revelation, you begin to see wealth through heaven's eyes. You see that prosperity is not about accumulation, but activation. It activates your generosity, your creativity, your compassion. It turns vision into action, dreams into institutions, ideas into impact. You start building not for applause, but for eternity.

The divine exchange is the place where grace meets responsibility. It is the holy tension between receiving freely and giving fully. It reminds you that nothing you offer to God is ever lost. Every seed sown in love returns in abundance, though not always in the form you expect. Sometimes it returns as peace. Sometimes as opportunities. Sometimes as souls saved through your obedience. The reward is always greater than the sacrifice.

Your life becomes a sermon without words when you live this way. People see the peace in your provision, the humility in your success, the generosity in your wealth. They see a different kind of prosperity, one that does not boast, but blesses. They see that your abundance has a pulse, because it is connected to the heart of God.

This is the kind of prosperity that transforms nations. When believers rise to live as stewards, not seekers, communities begin to change. Poverty loses its grip. Injustice weakens. Hope rises. The Kingdom expands, not through slogans or systems, but through hearts set on fire for divine purpose.

The divine exchange is not a moment; it is a lifestyle. It is waking each day with a renewed "yes" to God. It is choosing to trust when it is easier to control. It is giving when it feels uncomfortable. It is serving when it is inconvenient. It is believing that your greatest wealth is not in what you keep, but in what you release.

Divine Wealth

When your life becomes an offering, you begin to experience heaven on earth. You see miracles in motion, provision in unexpected places, joy in hidden corners. You realise that nothing you give to God ever diminishes you; it multiplies you. Every sacrifice becomes seed, every act of obedience becomes overflow.

And when all is said and done, when your journey reaches its final chapter, may you stand before your Creator and hear the words that make every labour worth it: "Well done, good and faithful servant." Not because you became rich in the world's eyes, but because you were faithful with what He gave you. Not because you built empires, but because you built people. Not because you gained, but because you gave.

You will see then what you cannot fully see now, that every prayer mattered, every gift multiplied, every act of faith wrote a line in God's eternal story. You will see that the exchange was never loss; it was transformation. You gave Him your effort, and He gave you His glory. You gave Him your time, and He gave you eternity. You gave Him your seed, and He gave you harvest beyond measure.

This is the divine exchange: the holy meeting point of heaven's abundance and human surrender. It is the place where faith becomes fruitfulness, and fruitfulness becomes worship. It is the revelation that true wealth is not found in possession, but in participation, in being part of what God is doing on the earth.

So take all that you have, and all that you are, and place it back in His hands. Let your wealth serve His will. Let your life become an offering. Let your work be worship. Let your legacy be light.

And as you do, heaven will respond with more than you could ever imagine, not because you asked for it, but because you became a vessel for it. This is abundance in its purest form. This is prosperity in its highest expression. This is divine wealth, God's way.

Divine Wealth

Epilogue: Walking It Out – Turning Divine Wealth into Real-World Income

Divine Wealth

There comes a moment when revelation must meet reality, when faith must take on feet. You have prayed, believed, fasted, and renewed your mind through the truths of Divine Wealth. You have learned to see abundance not as a selfish pursuit but as a sacred partnership with God. Now the question is, what will you do with that revelation? How do you move from believing in prosperity to building something that sustains it? The answer lies in understanding that faith without works is not incomplete; it is inactive. Real faith breathes through motion.

God does not bless our ideas in theory; He blesses them in action. When He gave the Israelites the Promised Land, He did not drop houses and vineyards from the sky. He gave them territory and expected them to occupy it. Likewise, God gives you potential and expects you to develop it. Your prosperity is not a miracle waiting to happen; it is a mission waiting to begin. Heaven will always supply the seed, but you must be willing to plant it.

Faith with Feet

Faith was never meant to stay confined to prayer rooms and vision boards. It was meant to show up in daily habits, financial decisions, business ideas, and creative pursuits. The God who created the world by speaking did not stop at words; He shaped the dust and breathed life into it. That is what He calls us to do, to take the breath of inspiration He gives and shape it into something tangible.

James reminds us that faith without works is dead. It is not that faith fails without works, but that it cannot fully live. Works are not the opposite of faith; they are its expression. When you begin to act on what you believe, heaven begins to move through you in ways you never imagined. The vision that once lived only in your heart becomes visible in your hands.

So as you reach this point in the journey, remember this: the goal of Divine Wealth is not just to think differently about abundance; it is to live differently because of it. True revelation always produces

Divine Wealth

transformation. The seed of understanding must now become a harvest of impact.

The Three Pillars of Practical Prosperity

Every believer who wants to manifest God's design for increase must understand three foundational pillars: purpose, planning, and production. These are not business theories; they are biblical principles seen in every story of divine success.

The first pillar is purpose. Purpose is what gives direction to abundance. Without it, wealth becomes wandering. You were not born to make money for money's sake; you were born to solve a divine problem. Somewhere in the world, there is a need that matches your gift. The reason God gave you talents, ideas, and passions is because he designed you to fill a gap that no one else can fill exactly the same way.

Purpose answers the question, "Why me?" When you discover that, money becomes a servant to mission rather than a master over your mind. People who live in purpose never chase wealth; they attract it, because provision follows purpose like a shadow follows light.

The second pillar is planning. Once purpose gives you direction, planning gives you structure. Even the most anointed vision will collapse without strategy. God himself models this principle. When he created the world, He did so in order. Day one built the foundation for day two. he spoke light before life because He knew nothing could grow without it. If the Creator uses structure, so should His children. Planning is not a lack of faith; it is an act of faith. It says, "I believe God will move, so I am preparing the ground."

The third pillar is production. Purpose and planning mean little without execution. God blesses what you build, not just what you dream. Production is where faith becomes fruit. It is the discipline of showing up, working diligently, and creating something that can serve others. Whether it is writing a book, starting a business, crafting a

Divine Wealth

product, or teaching a class, your production is your praise made visible. Heaven rejoices when you turn revelation into results.

Recognizing Your Seeds

One of the greatest keys to abundance is learning to recognize what is already in your hands. Many people pray for miracles while standing on the soil of their own answers. In 2 Kings 4, a widow cried out to the prophet Elisha, saying her debts were overwhelming and her sons were at risk of being taken as slaves. The prophet did not hand her gold; he asked her a question: "What do you have in your house?" She replied, "Nothing, except a small jar of oil." That "nothing" became everything. God multiplied what she already possessed once she recognized its value and obeyed His instruction.

The same is true for you. You may think what you have is insignificant, a skill, an idea, a bit of knowledge, but when placed in God's hands and activated by faith, it can become the beginning of your increase. Your "oil" might be your ability to teach, to write, to organize, to design, to cook, or to lead. It could be your story, your creativity, or your compassion. The key is to stop overlooking what heaven has already entrusted to you.

Take time to ask God, "What is in my house?" Identify your gifts, your passions, your resources, and your relationships. Every seed of greatness starts with recognition. You cannot multiply what you do not value, and you cannot value what you do not see.

Once you recognize your seeds, cultivate them. Invest time in developing your skills. Study, learn, and grow. God's anointing enhances excellence; it does not replace it. Preparation is not wasted time, it is worship. Every hour you spend refining your gift is a declaration of faith that says, "I am getting ready for increase."

Faith in Action: Modern Pathways to Prosperity

Today, the opportunities to create income are as diverse as the gifts God has given. You do not need to wait for permission or perfection to begin. You simply need to begin where you are. Faith moves best

Divine Wealth

when you take small, consistent steps in the direction of your purpose.

For some, this means using service-based skills to build income. Perhaps you have expertise in a particular area, teaching, consulting, mentoring, design, or administration. You can turn that into a business that blesses others while sustaining you. Remember, the Bible says a worker is worthy of their wages. Providing value to others is not greed; it is godly stewardship of your abilities.

For others, your path may involve creating products. That could mean writing a book, producing art, making handmade items, or designing resources that uplift and inspire. God is a Creator, and we reflect Him most when we create. Every product birthed from faith becomes a seed of influence in the world.

The digital economy has also opened doors that generations before us could not have imagined. The online space allows believers to share their gifts globally, through courses, podcasts, coaching, content creation, or online ministries. Your message can travel farther than your physical presence, reaching hearts across continents. You can earn income while expanding the Kingdom, proving that faith and innovation are not enemies but allies.

For others still, stewardship through investment may be their calling. Investing wisely is not unspiritual; it is strategic. The parable of the talents shows us that God expects increase, not idleness. Saving, buying property, supporting ethical ventures, or building partnerships that uplift communities are all ways to multiply resources with integrity.

Whatever form your pathway takes, remember this truth: God blesses movement. The moment you take a step, He multiplies it. The Red Sea did not part until Moses lifted his staff. The jar of oil did not flow until the widow poured. Miracles meet motion.

The Divine Business Model

Divine Wealth

Many believers feel torn between ministry and marketplace, as if they cannot serve God while building wealth. But Scripture shows us otherwise. The marketplace was God's idea. Jesus taught more parables about business and stewardship than about heaven itself because He knew that financial wisdom is a form of discipleship. The goal is not to build an empire for self, but to build a platform for service.

Operating a business or creative venture in alignment with God's principles begins with integrity. Your character must be the foundation upon which all profit is built. Without integrity, success becomes fragile. With it, your influence becomes enduring. Excellence, honesty, and consistency are acts of worship when offered to God.

Start small, but start well. You do not need to have everything figured out. Many great visions began as side projects of obedience. A small blog becomes a ministry. A tiny business becomes a global outreach. God multiplies what you steward with diligence and humility. The key is to start where you are, use what you have, and trust Him to expand it.

Planning is part of this divine business model. Write your vision and make it plain, just as Habakkuk instructed. Set goals, budgets, and timelines, but leave room for God's timing. Pray before decisions, seek wise counsel, and track your progress. Faith does not mean operating blindly; it means operating boldly.

Finally, generosity must remain central. Every time your business or creative effort grows, let giving grow with it. Make generosity part of your brand. The Kingdom advances when believers channel their wealth toward transformation. Whether it is funding missions, helping families, or creating opportunities for others, generosity keeps the flow of blessing alive. God will always entrust more to those who keep the river open.

Breaking Financial Fear

Divine Wealth

Perhaps the biggest barrier to abundance is fear. Fear of failure, fear of rejection, fear of not being "spiritual enough" to succeed. These fears disguise themselves as humility, but they are rooted in doubt. Fear whispers that you are not ready or that it is too risky to step out. But remember this: God has not given you the spirit of fear, but of power, love, and a sound mind.

You will never feel completely ready to walk in purpose. Faith begins where comfort ends. If you wait until everything feels safe, you will wait forever. God's promises are unlocked in obedience, not certainty. When Peter stepped out of the boat, the water did not become solid before his foot touched it; it became solid because he stepped. The same will be true for you. The moment you act in faith, provision will meet you.

Fear often hides behind perfectionism. You may tell yourself that you are waiting until you have enough experience or resources, but what you are really waiting for is the absence of risk. Yet faith requires risk. It requires trust in the unseen. God does not call the prepared; He prepares the called.

The way to overcome fear is to replace it with movement. Start small but start now. Make the call, write the idea, open the account, launch the page, record the message. Every small act of faith weakens fear's hold. Remember that courage is not the absence of fear; it is the decision to move despite it.

Stewardship Systems

Once you have overcome fear and begun to act on your purpose, you must learn to build systems that sustain it. Blessing without structure becomes burden. Many people pray for increase but do not prepare for it. They want overflow, yet have no container to hold it. Stewardship is the art of creating those containers.

Financial stewardship begins with clarity. You cannot manage what you do not measure. Create a simple plan for every resource God entrusts to you. Know where your money goes, and give every dollar

Divine Wealth

an assignment. This is not about control; it is about accountability. Even in Scripture, when Jesus multiplied the loaves and fish, He told the disciples to gather the leftovers so that nothing would be wasted. That was stewardship.

Budgeting, saving, and investing are not unspiritual practices; they are sacred disciplines. They are acts of obedience that show God you can handle more. A budget does not limit you; it liberates you. It allows you to see clearly what God has already provided and how it can be multiplied. Saving is not about fear; it is about foresight. Joseph saved grain during abundance so that a nation could survive famine. Preparation was his prophecy.

Beyond financial systems, stewardship includes managing time, energy, and relationships. Wealth is not only measured in money but in moments, connections, and wisdom. How you spend your hours will determine how you experience abundance. Every seed of greatness requires the soil of focus. Eliminate distractions that drain your energy and invest your attention in the assignments that build fruit.

Relationships, too, are a form of currency. Surround yourself with people who stretch your vision, not shrink it. Seek mentors who can guide you in wisdom and peers who will hold you accountable. Scripture says iron sharpens iron, and that principle applies to every season of growth. God often answers prayers for provision by sending people, not things. Steward those relationships with gratitude and discernment.

Giving as a Lifestyle

As you grow in abundance, never forget the foundation of all prosperity: generosity. Giving is not a one-time act; it is a lifestyle. It is the posture of a heart that understands everything belongs to God. When you give, you do not lose; you invest in eternity. You keep the divine circulation of blessing alive.

Divine Wealth

Many people stop giving when they begin building wealth, believing they must secure their foundation first. But in the Kingdom, giving is the foundation. It keeps your heart soft and your perspective pure. It reminds you that God is your source, not your income. When you give from a place of joy and trust, you open doors that calculation never could. remains true: "Give, and it will be given to you, good measure, pressed down, shaken together, and running over." Generosity is also a business principle. The most successful entrepreneurs, ministries, and creators understand the law of sowing and reaping. When you add value, serve others, and bless those around you, the flow of provision never ceases. God can always trust hands that remain open. Make generosity part of your system, not just your emotion. Plan your giving the same way you plan your spending. Give strategically, faithfully, and cheerfully. The result will be supernatural sustainability.

The Power of Excellence

As you build, never underestimate the power of excellence. In the world's systems, people often pursue shortcuts. But the Kingdom operates on quality. Excellence is not perfection; it is devotion. It means doing ordinary things with extraordinary care because you are doing them for God. says, "Whatever you do, work at it with all your heart, as working for the Lord, not for human masters."

Excellence attracts divine favor and human trust. It opens doors that prayer alone cannot open. When people see your work reflect integrity, diligence, and beauty, they see the reflection of God in you. Whether you are creating a product, leading a team, or offering a service, do it as worship. Every detail matters because it speaks of your Creator.

When Daniel served in Babylon, his excellence distinguished him from others. He rose to positions of influence not by compromise but by consistency. Excellence became his evangelism. In the same

Divine Wealth

way, your diligence and creativity can become a testimony that draws people to God.

Turning Purpose into Income

Let us talk plainly about money. There is no conflict between spirituality and profitability when purpose leads the way. Wealth creation is not a sin; it is a strategy. God uses resources to amplify your reach and fulfill His work through you.

Begin by identifying how your gifts meet real needs. Every problem you solve holds value. Every idea that improves a life deserves compensation. That is not greed; that is stewardship. Jesus said the worker is worthy of their wages, which means it is righteous to receive for what you contribute.

If you are a teacher, you can build courses that share your wisdom. If you are a writer, your words can create passive income streams. If you have a skill, you can serve others through coaching or consulting. If you have creativity, you can design products, art, or media that carry your message. The internet has made it possible for purpose-driven people to prosper without compromising their faith.

Do not despise small beginnings. Every stream starts as a drop. Create one product, offer one service, start one platform, and nurture it. Consistency compounds. Over time, what begins as a single step of faith becomes a flow of provision. The key is to build with integrity and persistence. Wealth grows when you water it with patience.

Building a Legacy Mindset

Abundance is not complete until it multiplies beyond you. Legacy wealth is not just about inheritance; it is about impact. It is what remains when you are no longer present. The Bible says a good person leaves an inheritance for their children's children. That inheritance is not only financial; it is spiritual, intellectual, and moral. It is the wisdom you pass down, the habits you model, and the systems you build.

Divine Wealth

Ask yourself: what will continue because I was faithful? Legacy is built one decision at a time, through consistent giving, wise investment, and intentional mentorship. Teach others what you learn. Share knowledge freely. Raise others to rise with you. When your success lifts others, your legacy becomes eternal.

Think generationally. Plan not just for profit but for purpose that lasts. Set up systems that can outlive you, charitable foundations, scholarships, community projects, or businesses that continue serving after you are gone. The Kingdom of God advances when believers think beyond their lifespan.

Living in Divine Partnership

As you move into tangible abundance, remember that everything you build remains a partnership between you and God. Prosperity becomes dangerous when it becomes self-centered. Stay anchored in prayer and humility. Continue to seek God's direction in every decision. He is the architect; you are the builder. When you keep Him at the center, He will guide your steps with wisdom beyond your experience.

Invite God into your strategy sessions, not just your Sunday prayers. Ask Him for insight before launching projects or making investments. The Holy Spirit is the best business partner you will ever have. He gives ideas, reveals opportunities, and warns of traps. Spiritual sensitivity is your greatest competitive advantage in a world driven by noise.

Never separate your devotion from your ambition. Let them merge. Your work is an altar when your motive is worship. As says, "Commit to the Lord whatever you do, and He will establish your plans." When your plans align with His purpose, success becomes inevitable.

The Power of Rest and Rhythm

Abundance is not achieved through exhaustion but through rhythm. Even in creation, God worked for six days and rested on the seventh.

Divine Wealth

That rhythm was His design for sustainability. Burnout is not a badge of faithfulness; it is a sign of imbalance. To keep creating, you must keep resting. Rest is not idleness; it is renewal.

Rest allows God to refresh your creativity and restore your clarity. It reminds you that you are not the source, He is. Schedule time to breathe, reflect, and celebrate what God has done. Gratitude keeps your heart aligned with grace. When you rest in trust, your work carries peace instead of pressure.

Commissioning the Reader

As you reach this point, pause and look at what you have learned. You now know that abundance begins in the spirit but manifests through strategy. You understand that faith must move, that purpose must produce, and that stewardship sustains. You have seen that wealth is not worldly when it serves godly purpose. You are equipped to walk into your own divine economy.

But knowledge alone will not change your story. Action will. God is waiting for your obedience, not your perfection. Every great journey begins with one step. The next chapter of your life is not written by fear but by faith that moves. You are capable of creating, building, and giving in ways that reflect heaven on earth.

So here is your commissioning:

Step out and build. Write the vision. Launch the idea. Plant the seed. Start the business. Create the product. Mentor the next person. Use your hands as instruments of worship and your work as a testimony of God's faithfulness.

When you move, heaven moves. When you give, the flow continues. When you build with love, what you build will last. You are not just called to believe in abundance; you are called to embody it. You are the evidence that God still blesses obedience.

Declare these words with faith:

"I am a vessel of divine abundance. I am a steward of God's increase. Everything I touch prospers because it serves His purpose. I walk in

Divine Wealth

wisdom, I work in excellence, and I give with joy. My life is a reflection of God's provision, and through me, His Kingdom will advance."

That is your truth. That is your assignment. That is the tangible expression of Divine Wealth, faith that moves, wisdom that builds, and generosity that transforms.

Now, go and live it. Build boldly, give freely, and rest deeply. Let your life become a living testimony that heaven's blueprint still works on earth.

Divine Wealth

About the Author

The author chooses to remain unnamed, serving only as a vessel through which truth and inspiration may flow. This book is not about who the writer is, but about what readers can become through faith, wisdom, and purpose. Each chapter was written in prayerful reflection, inspired during moments of offering and tithing.

The intention is simple: that every reader who is blessed by this message will use the insight gained to create increase and then return that increase as offering—a continuous cycle of giving and growth. May this work remind you that all abundance begins with gratitude and flows through generosity.

May it move you not just to believe, but to build, and to give in ways that glorify the Source of all provision.

www.ingramcontent.com/pod-product-compliance
Lightning Source LLC
LaVergne TN
LVHW051519070426
835507LV00023B/3200